SAMHAIN

Llewellyn's Sabbat Essentials

SAMHAIN

Rituals, Recipes & Lore for Halloween

Llewellyn Publications
Woodbury, Minnesota

FIRST EDITION
Seventeenth Printing, 2023

Book design: Donna Burch-Brown
Cover art: iStockphoto.com/18232461/©Electric_Crayon
        iStockphoto.com/8926216/©Anna-Lena
        iStockphoto.com/10848596/©nicoolay
        iStockphoto.com/14009704/©LoopAll
Cover design: Kevin R. Brown
Interior illustrations: Mickie Mueller

Llewellyn Publications is a registered trademark of Llewellyn Worldwide Ltd.

Library of Congress Cataloging-in-Publication Data
Rajchel, Diana.
  Samhain rituals, recipes, and lore for Halloween / by Diana Rajchel.
— First Edition.
      pages cm. — (Llewellyn's sabbat essentials ; #6)
  Includes bibliographical references and index.
  ISBN 978-0-7387-4216-8
1. Samhain. I. Title.
  BF1572.S35R35 2015
  299'.94—dc23
                              2015005468

Llewellyn Publications
A Division of Llewellyn Worldwide Ltd.
2143 Wooddale Drive
Woodbury, MN 55125-2989
www.llewellyn.com

Contents

...th bereavement, and ancestry, courage, beginnings, endings, ch

arnation, wisdom, survival, preservation, hunting, other worlds,

ing, release from old bonds, road openings, fire, protection sun

of scorpio, sun sign of scorpio, dark moon, pleiades at highe

at midnight, the crone, the grieving mother, the grieving wife,

eter, Persephone and Hades, Ereshkigal, Osiris, Janus, Cer

munnos, the Daghda, Hecate, Dis Pater, Hel, Inanna,

Lilith, Macha, Mare, the Morrigan, Osiris, Isis,

Rhiannon, Samana, Teutates, Taranis, the Horned God, t

orange, brown, yellow, grey, green, cedar, dittany of crete, sag

corn, wheat, rye, pumpkins, hazel, hemlock, chrysanthemum, ca

igold, jet, obsidian, onyx, carnelian, moonstone, iron, black

rs, owls, ravens, decaying leaves, myrrh, copal, death, wheel of

igh priestess, cauldron, mask, besom, apple, pumpkin, fermented

raut, pickled eggs, pickled beets, roasted nuts, raw nuts, app

wool, divination, soul cakes, sugar skulls, jack-o-lanterns, b

bobbing, seances, scrying, bonfires, trick-or-treating, mummer

off gravesites, dedicate memorials, visit nursing homes, sam

olan gael, colan gael, oidhche a mhadhain, colan gael, oidh

LLEWELLYN'S SABBAT ESSENTIALS

LLEWELLYN'S SABBAT ESSENTIALS provides instruction and inspiration for honoring each of the modern witch's sabbats. Packed with spells, rituals, meditations, history, lore, invocations, divination, recipes, crafts, and more, each book in this eight volume series explores both the old and new ways of celebrating the seasonal rites that act as cornerstones in the witch's year.

There are eight sabbats, or holidays, celebrated by Wiccans and many other Neopagans (modern Pagans) today. Together, these eight sacred days make up what's known as the Wheel of the Year, or the sabbat cycle, with each sabbat corresponding to an important turning point in nature's annual journey through the seasons.

Devoting our attention to the Wheel of the Year allows us to better attune ourselves to the energetic cycles of nature and listen to what each season is whispering (or shouting!) to us, rather than working against the natural tides. What better time to start new projects than as the earth reawakens after a long winter, and suddenly everything is blooming and growing and shooting up out of the ground again? And what better time to meditate and plan ahead than during the introspective slumber of winter? With Llewellyn's Sabbat Essentials, you'll learn how to focus on the spiritual aspects of the Wheel of the Year, how to move through it and with it in harmony, and how to celebrate your own ongoing growth and achievements. This may be your first book on Wicca, Witchcraft, or Paganism, or your newest addition to a bookcase or e-reader already crammed with magickal wisdom. In either case, we hope you will find something of value here to take with you on your journey.

Take a Trip Through the Wheel of the Year

The eight sabbats each mark an important point in nature's annual cycles. They are depicted as eight evenly spaced spokes on a wheel representing the year as a whole; the dates on which they fall are nearly evenly spaced on the calendar, as well.

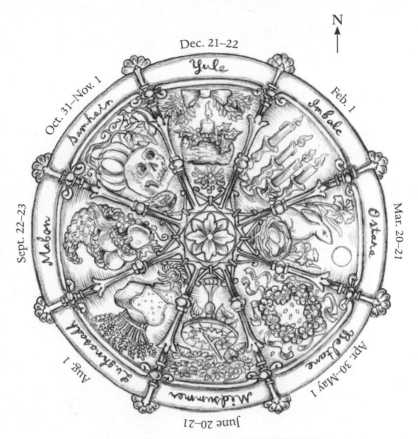

N

Dec. 21–22

Yule

Oct. 31–Nov. 1

Samhain

Feb. 1

Imbolc

Sept. 22–23

Mabon

Mar. 20–21

Ostara

Aug. 1

Lughnasadh

Apr. 30–May 1

Beltane

Midsummer

June 20–21

Wheel of the Year—Northern Hemisphere
(All solstice and equinox dates are approximate,
and one should consult an almanac or a calendar
to find the correct dates each year.)

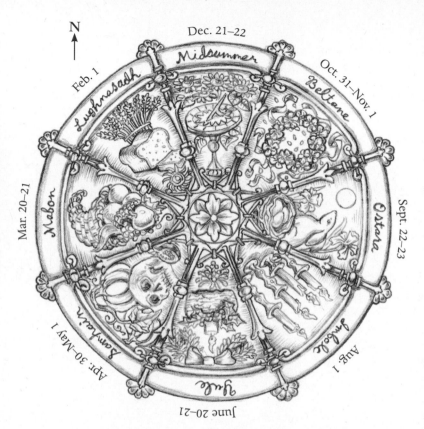

Wheel of the Year—Southern Hemisphere

The Wheel is comprised of two groups of four holidays each. There are four solar festivals relating to the sun's position in the sky, dividing the year into quarters: the Spring Equinox, the Summer Solstice, the Fall Equinox, and the Winter Solstice, all of which are dated astronomically and thus vary slightly from year to year. Falling in between these quarter days are the cross-quarter holidays, or fire festivals: Imbolc, Beltane, Lughnasadh, and Samhain. The quarters are sometimes called the Lesser Sabbats and the cross-quarters the Greater Sabbats, although neither cycle is "superior" to the other. In the Southern Hemisphere, seasons are opposite those in the north, and the sabbats are consequently celebrated at different times.

While the book you are holding only focuses on Samhain, it can be helpful to know how it fits in with the cycle as a whole.

The Winter Solstice, also called Yule or Midwinter, occurs when nighttime has reached its maximum length; after the solstice, the length of the days will begin to increase. Though the cold darkness is upon us, there is a promise of brighter days to come. In Wiccan lore, this is the time when the young solar god is born. In some Neopagan traditions, this is when the Holly King is destined to lose the battle to his lighter aspect, the Oak King. Candles are lit, feasts are enjoyed, and evergreen foliage is brought in the house as a reminder that, despite the harshness of winter, light and life have endured.

At Imbolc (also spelled Imbolg), the ground is just starting to thaw, signaling that it's time to start preparing the fields for the approaching sowing season. We begin to awaken from our months of introspection and start to sort out what we have learned over that time, while also taking the first steps to make plans for our future. Some Wiccans also bless candles at Imbolc, another symbolic way of coaxing along the now perceptibly stronger light.

On the Spring Equinox, also known as Ostara, night and day are again equal in length, and following this, the days will grow longer than the nights. The Spring Equinox is a time of renewal, a time to plant seeds as the earth once again comes to life. We decorate eggs as a symbol of hope, life, and fertility, and we perform rituals to energize ourselves so that we can find the power and passion to live and grow.

In agricultural societies, Beltane marked the start of the summer season. Livestock were led out to graze in abundant pastures and trees burst into beautiful and fragrant blossom. Rituals were performed to protect crops, livestock, and people. Fires were lit and offerings were made in the hopes of gaining divine protection. In Wiccan mythos, the young god impregnates the young goddess. We all have something we want to harvest by the end of the year—plans we are determined to realize—and Beltane is a great time to enthusiastically get that process in full swing.

The Summer Solstice is the longest day of the year. It's also called Litha, or Midsummer. Solar energies are at their apex, and the power of nature is at its height. In Wiccan lore, it's the time when the solar god's power is at its greatest (so, paradoxically, his power must now start to decrease), having impregnated the maiden goddess, who then transforms into the earth mother.

In some Neopagan traditions, this is when the Holly King once again battles his lighter aspect, this time vanquishing the Oak King. It's generally a time of great merriment and celebration.

At Lughnasadh, the major harvest of the summer has ripened. Celebrations are held, games are played, gratitude is expressed, and feasts are enjoyed. Also known as Lammas, this is the time we celebrate the first harvest—whether that means the first of our garden crops or the first of our plans that have come to fruition. To celebrate the grain harvest, bread is often baked on this day.

The Autumn Equinox, also called Mabon, marks another important seasonal change and a second harvest. The sun shines equally on both hemispheres, and the lengths of night and day are equal. After this point, the nights will again be longer than the days. In connection with the harvest, the day is celebrated as a festival of sacrifice and of the dying god, and tribute is paid to the sun and the fertile earth.

To the Celtic people, Samhain marked the start of the winter season. It was the time when the livestock was slaughtered and the final harvest was gathered before the inevitable plunge into the depths of winter's darkness. Fires were lit to help wandering spirits on their way, and offerings were given in the names of the gods and the ancestors. Seen as a beginning, Samhain is now often called the Witches' New Year. We honor our ancestors, wind down our activities, and get ready for the months of introspection ahead ... and the cycle continues.

The Modern Pagan's Relationship to the Wheel

Modern Pagans take inspiration from many pre-Christian spiritual traditions, exemplified by the Wheel of the Year. The cycle of eight festivals we recognize throughout modern Pagandom today was never celebrated in full by any one particular pre-Christian culture. In the 1940s and 1950s, a British man named Gerald Gardner created the new religion of Wicca by drawing on a variety of cultures and traditions, deriving and adapting practices from pre-Christian religion, animistic beliefs, folk magick, and various shamanic disciplines and esoteric orders. He combined multicultural equinox and solstice traditions with Celtic feast days and early European agricultural and pastoral celebrations to create a single model that became the framework for the Wiccan ritual year.

This Wiccan ritual year is popularly followed by Wiccans and witches, as well as many eclectic Pagans of various stripes. Some Pagans only observe half of the sabbats, either the quarters or the cross-quarters. Other Pagans reject the Wheel of the Year altogether and follow a festival calendar based on the culture of whatever specific path they follow rather than a nature-based agrarian cycle. We all have such unique paths in Paganism that it is important not to make any assumptions about another's based on your own; maintaining an open and positive attitude is what makes the Pagan community thrive.

Many Pagans localize the Wheel of the Year to their own environment. Wicca has grown to become a truly global religion, but few of us live in a climate mirroring Wicca's British Isles origins. While traditionally Imbolc is the beginning of the thaw and the awakening of the earth, it is the height of winter in many northern climes. While Lammas may be a grateful celebration of the harvest for some, in areas prone to drought and forest fires it is a dangerous and uncertain time of year.

There are also the two hemispheres to consider. While it's winter in the Northern Hemisphere, it's summer in the Southern Hemisphere. While Pagans in America are celebrating Yule and the Winter Solstice, Pagans in Australia are celebrating Midsummer. The practitioner's own lived experiences are more important than any dogma written in a book when it comes to observing the sabbats.

In that spirit, you may wish to delay or move up celebrations so that the seasonal correspondences better fit your own locale, or you may emphasize different themes for each sabbat as you experience it. This series should make such options easily accessible to you.

No matter what kind of place you live on the globe, be it urban, rural, or suburban, you can adapt sabbat traditions and practices to suit your own life and environment. Nature is all around us; no matter how hard we humans try to insulate ourselves from nature's cycles, these recurring seasonal changes are inescapable. Instead of swimming against the tide, many modern Pagans embrace each season's unique energies, whether dark, light, or in between, and integrate these energies into aspects of our own everyday lives.

Llewellyn's Sabbat Essentials series offers all the information you need in order to do just that. Each book will resemble the one you hold in your hands. The first chapter, *Old Ways*, shares the history and lore that have been passed down, from mythology and pre-Christian traditions to any vestiges still seen in modern life. *New Ways* then spins those themes and elements into the manners in which modern Pagans observe and celebrate the sabbat. The next chapter focuses on *Spells and Divination* appropriate to the season or based in folklore, while the following one, *Recipes and Crafts*, offers ideas for decorating your home, hands-on crafts, and recipes that take advantage of seasonal offerings. The chapter *Prayers and Invocations* provides ready-made calls and prayers you may use in ritual, meditation, or journaling. The *Rituals of Celebration* chapter provides three complete rituals: one for a solitary, one for two people, and one for a whole group such as a coven, circle, or grove. (Feel free to adapt each or any ritual to your own needs, substituting your own offerings, calls, invocations, magickal workings, and so on. When planning a group ritual, try to be conscious of any special needs participants may have. There are many wonderful books available that delve into the fine points of facilitating ritual if you don't have experience in this department.) Finally, in the back of the book you'll find a complete list of correspondences for the holiday, from magickal themes to deities to foods, colors, symbols, and more.

By the end of this book you'll have the knowledge and the inspiration to celebrate the sabbat with gusto. By honoring the Wheel of the Year, we reaffirm our connection to nature so that as her endless cycles turn, we're able to go with the flow and enjoy the ride.

OLD WAYS

...rnation, wisdom, survival, preservation, hunting, other worlds,

...ng, release from old bonds, road openings, fire, protection sun

...of scorpio, sun sign of scorpio, dark moon, pleiades at highes...

...at midnight, the crone, the grieving mother, the grieving wife, t...

...er, Persephone and Hades, Ereshkigal, Osiris, Janus, Cerr...

...muinos, the Daghda, Hecate, Dis Pater, Hel, Inanna, Is...

..., Lilith, Macha, Mare, the Morrigan, Osiris, Isis, Pa...

Rhiannon, Samana, Teutates, Taranis, the Horned God, the...

orange-brown, yellow, grey, green, cedar, dittany of crete, sage...

...orn, wheat, rye, pumpkins, hazel, hemlock, chrysanthemum, cal...

...rigold, jet, obsidian, onyx, carnelian, moonstone, iron, black c...

...s, owls, ravens, decaying leaves, myrrh, copal, death, wheel of y...

...h priestess, cauldron, mask, besom, apple, pumpkin, fermented...

...raut, pickled eggs, pickled beets, roasted nuts, raw nuts, appl...

...wool, divination, soul cakes, sugar skulls, jack-o-lanterns, ba...

...bobbing, seances, scrying, bonfires, trick-or-treating, mummer...

...n off gravesites, dedicate memorials, visit nursing homes, sam...

...alan gaef, calan gaef, gealach a ruadhain, calan gaef, hala-y...

*A*T SAMHAIN, THE circle of the year has come to its final spoke in the Wheel. At this time, the harvest has finished, the dying god interred, and the goddess has descended to the underworld to be with her beloved. Above, her people prepare for the veil between the worlds to thin; dead ancestors will be visiting, and with the harvest tools put away, there's a new year to think about, resources to manage, goodbyes to say, and plans to make. Meanwhile, the now barren land gives way to the rulership of the Crone.

In some climates, October is a sad and beautiful time. Autumn leaves cover the ground like bright bleeding, leaving the trees bare. The grass fades from green to brown and in mornings carries the white hoar of frost. The temperatures grow colder, forcing more and more time indoors, and with what we have gathered, we have just a bit more time to remember the loved ones we no longer have. Many Pagans believe a membranelike veil separates the world of spirit from the physical world and that it thins the most in late autumn. Things pass through that membrane. Those things might be spirits, faeries, or even the departed ones we wish so much to see again. This veil also makes Samhain season ideal for magick and divination.

Halloween coincides with Samhain. Consequently, many Pagans see Halloween as half of the whole celebration. This time of costumes, revelry, and social inversion grew from the same traditional roots. Samhain is serious and loving—Grandma might visit—while Halloween releases our restrained wildness. Many Pagans revere both agricultural cycles and the processes of nature; this dichotomy manifests in this sometimes two-sided celebration. Both the reverent and the silly have their place on October 31.

Samhain is Gaelic and usually pronounced SOW-win. Most Gaelic speakers translate it to mean "summer's end." In the early twentieth century, some scholars argued that the name for the holiday came from the word *samhtheine*, meaning "fire of peace" (MacLean). Modern Celtic and Druidic Pagans may have several other names for this day as well, depending on the flavor of their Celtic roots. The Welsh may call it *Calan Gaeaf* (or *Nos Calan Gaeaf*), and the Manx *Oie Houney* or *Hop-tu-naa*. The Welsh, Scottish, and Irish customs were often about ensuring home and hearth had protection through the winter. The Manx saw (and still see) *Oie Houney* as a new year celebration. These are not all the same holidays as Samhain exactly—but perhaps around this time of year with the veil so thin, the division of meaning and practice between different cultures thins as well.

For modern populist Pagans, all these old and still living festivals inform the meaning of their own celebrations.

The Fire Festival

To the ancient Celts, Samhain marked the most important of four Celtic fire festivals. Located halfway between an equinox and a solstice, it is one of four cross-quarter festivals. Every year on the first frost after the full moon in October, families allowed their hearth fires to burn out. At this time, they brought back herd animals from grazing and completed gathering the harvest.

After the fires died, they gathered with the rest of their tribe to observe the Druid priests relighting the community sacred fire using friction. The priests induced friction with a wheel and spindle: the wheel, representing the sun, turned from east to west and lit sparks. At this time, they made prayers and offerings or sacrifices related to their needs. The *Crom-cruach* came out: this was an emblem of the sun, and scholars are uncertain whether it represented a Pagan god or symbolized an aspect of nature embodied in a stone pillar.

The villagers left offerings of food at the edge of their village for wandering spirits and faerie folk. There was also a sacrifice of a black sheep, a black sow, or cattle. At the end, every person returned home with a brand lit from the sacred fire, which they used to relight their own hearth and then to light bonfires or to set torches at the edge of their fields. These ancients considered it a sin to relight the hearth fire any other way.

To the ancient Celts, Samhain marked the completion of the harvest and called them to put their energy into preparing for the coming winter. It also betokened a day when their ancestors would come to visit, followed across the veil by all sorts of creatures both good and bad that moved freely in the mortal world on Samhain night. Since faeries were often unfriendly, the Celts dressed themselves as animals or as other fearsome creatures as a way to prevent kidnapping by faeries and later by witches.

The Christian Influence

When Christianity spread throughout Europe, the church officials went about converting the area heathens by converting their holidays. Sometimes church officials did this by scheduling an observance for a different time of year. Other times, they simply renamed the old Pagan holiday for a saint's day. In the fifth century, Pope Boniface attempted to repurpose the ritual of honoring otherworldly spirits and the dead, identifying it as a day to honor saints and martyrs, and moving the holiday to May 13.

When the late October/November fire festivals continued anyway, in the ninth-century Pope Gregory decided to move the saints and martyrs day back to the same day as the secular festival of the dead. In the case of Samhain, rather than negate the festival of the dead, the church resorted to declaring November 1 All Saints' Day, alternatively called All Souls' Day. Later the church added All Souls' Day on November 2, possibly because All Saints' Day failed to displace the Pagan rituals.

Eventually both All Saints' and All Souls' became distinct holidays unto themselves, with All Saints' an observance for souls believed already ascended to heaven, and All Souls' as a day to honor souls possibly still working out some issues in purgatory. In Ireland, these days marked a time for family reunions after cow-milking season finished. Over time the night before November 1, called among many names Hallowe'en, Allhallows eve, or Hallowmas, became the repository for most of the original Pagan practices.

The Export of Hallowe'en

When the Ulster Protestants (Ireland) settled in the United States in the nineteenth century, they brought their own Samhain/Halloween traditions along. They had parties, games, and masquerade parades, and their non-Irish neighbors joined the revelry. Most of what the other colonists adopted was the tradition of parties and games for children. Older children and young adults could attend these parties as part of local courtship practices.

In the 1930s, the tradition of Halloween pranking became a significant and expensive problem in many American communities. By 1950, most cities had some type of trick-or-treating event as a way of distracting the troublemakers.

Halloween caught on in the United States as a commercial event around 1970, when it stopped serving only as a holiday to entertain children and became a secular holiday for everyone. The LGBT community in New York adopted the holiday as a day to celebrate their true selves, college students began having costume parties and trick-a-shot events, and companies began producing paper-wrapped candy and house decorations.

As Halloween became prevalent in the United States, it also became more controversial. Some Christians aware of its Pagan origins objected strenuously to expanded observation of the holiday in the United States. People in rural areas especially referred to Halloween by the derogatory "Beggar's Night" as they saw it as door-to-door panhandling and sometimes extortion. The tradition of pranking as currently practiced is generally just base destruction, uncreative on the part of the vandals and expensive on the part of its victims.

The Reassertion of Samhain

In truth, Samhain changed costumes more than it disappeared. By 1980, as the Pagan movement in North America and the Wiccan and Traditional Witch movement in the United Kingdom grew, more people began practicing serious and solemn celebrations on October 31 or on the full moon closest to it. Many in the United Kingdom never really stopped practicing the old Samhain traditions, embedded as they were in the folk culture of their communities. Pagans who now observe the holiday often practice modernized versions, complete with horror movies, trick-or-treating, and pumpkin carving. Others prefer a solemn observation. Many specific traditions of Paganism may have their own prescribed practices for the day, as well.

The veil bleeds thin at Samhain, and that very small, soft line between secular and spirit especially shows in the meaning behind medieval and more modern Samhain practices. In the end, many of the traditions of this holiday that appear Pagan are actually embedded in Christian lore, such as trick-or-treating, whereas the seemingly Christian practices, such as honoring the dead, have a deeper connection to the old Pagan lore. Many of these deep-rooted ancient practices also make appearances, sometimes in new forms, in modern Pagan tradition.

Night Lights

The Celtic fire festival took on new expressions in the Middle Ages, some of which are still practiced well into the modern day. For instance, in Wales and the Scottish Highlands, servants and boys from around age eight into their teens would go to a bonfire built at the main street of the village, light torches, and run to field and farm, planting the torches at the boundaries of their properties. Families and communities might then build bonfires on hills close to their farms. These bonfires, called *samghnagans,* kicked off the land rituals of those nights. The intention, according to the Welsh, was to scare off faeries. In later years, they said it protected their farms and homes from witchcraft.

For those who went out into the night, they carried carved turnips on strings with a glowing piece of coal inside. These lanterns, called jack-o'-lanterns, came to refer to a Christian legend about a blacksmith named Old Jack—a man so evil that both heaven and hell refused him. With nowhere to go but purgatory, he had to roam the roads on Hallowe'en night with nothing but a turnip lamp to light his way. When Hallowe'en observances came to the New World, pumpkins were more common than turnips, so the Irish settlers used those for their lanterns instead.

Often the men of Wales might stay out at the bonfires also lit on hilltops on Halloween night, throwing firebrands at each other, engaging in somewhat violent games, and lighting off fireworks. When the fires burned out, they ran down the hills shouting. In the northern parts of Great Britain, sometimes they also carried noisemakers, such as bells and horns, that they played as they ran.

Over time, the rituals for protection from faeries changed to protection from "witchcraft." In Victorian times, villagers would throw an effigy of an old woman into the flames and call that "burning the witch."

Welsh communities also enacted a Halloween ritual called a Tinley. After the fires in town centers or on farms burned down, every member of that community placed a stone in the ashes, forming a circle. If a person found his or her stone moved the next morning, the community considered this person claimed by the fey, and expected him or her to die within the coming year. For all the seeming superstition, these rituals also had a practical benefit—the fire and ash protected fields from invasive plants the following year.

The Irish, on the other hand, put out their hearth fires on Samhain and used candles in the evening instead. Women of the house would make candles for each of her neighbors. She would give them to her neighbors to pray over, and pray for her neighbors over the candles given to her.

Lighting the Way for the Ancestors

The torches of the Welsh and the jack-o'-lanterns left at the edge of walks "kept witches away," but they also lit a path for ancestors wandering across the veil. Candles might be placed in windows—usually in the west, to represent the land of the dead—or lights placed along walkways and paths so that the beloved dead visiting from across the veil could find the way to the door of their loved ones' homes.

The Celts considered it unlucky to let a hearth fire go out on Samhain night. It meant darker events awaited them in the coming year.

Feeding the Dead

This night also called for a "dumb supper" or similar acts of feeding dead ancestors that might cross from the veil—or purgatory—for a visit. During these events, people set out food for their family and for their departed ancestors. Participants consumed these meals either in silence or in muted tones, except at the beginning of the ceremony, when they invited ancestors, and at the end when they bid the ancestors to leave.

In Ireland, families left the doors and windows unlocked, and set out cakes saved for the visiting dead. Any mortal who ate it was guilty of sacrilege and was condemned to afterlife as a hungry ghost. After the meal, the dead apparently expected entertainment, so children played games related to the rituals of Samhain while the adults discussed the events of the previous year for the ancestors to hear.

This tradition also came to Colonial and post-Colonial United States, where it became an overt superstitious magickal practice. The version reported by one group of Kentucky folklorists stated that the supper was prepared in silence, but that those making it also walked backward the entire time, and when possible prepared the food with their hands positioned behind their backs (Lindsey). No one would eat until a sign, ostensibly supernatural, appeared, such as two men carrying a corpse or a large white dog.

The Fearsome Things

While the early Celtic Christians invented Old Jack, the British Isles had other monsters to fear tracing back to their Pagan days. Yet others reflected the evolving political history of the Isles. Early on, people carried lanterns on Samhain night and went out in groups lest they run into any of a host of wicked characters. They might run afoul of a Pucah (or Pookah) a shapeshifting faery prone to both seduction and outright kidnapping. This was far from the only lurking shadow.

The Lady Gwyn (or Wen) was a woman who appeared dressed in white, sometimes headless and evil, sometimes playing the role of a benign lost soul. Similar to many spirits associated with Allhallows, she chased travelers she caught wandering in the night. A popular folk song describes this lady:

> *A tail-less Black Sow and a White Lady without a head*
> *May the tail-less black sow snatch the hindmost.*
> *A tail-less black sow on winter's eve,*
> *Thieves coming along knitting stockings. (Howard)*

This seemingly nonsensical verse may combine forgotten goddess images with water spirit images. Different folktales about white ladies and about *the* White Lady appear throughout the British Isles. In one story, a man, seeing her in distress, asks her if he can help, and she asks him to hold on to her hands until she tells him to stop and her troubles would leave her. A barking dog distracted the man so he let go her hands—she disappeared, crying that she was bound for yet another seven years. In a gentler legend, a farmer saw a woman in white scattering rose petals in a sheep's meadow. When she left, he gathered the flowers. The next day, the flowers disappeared, but he found three gold coins in their place (Hope).

In addition to these tales of enchantment, more frightening/less benign White Lady stories appear in different locales throughout Great Britain. In many of these tales, her character is a tragic figure—victim of murder or suicide—or is a guardian of treasure. In other stories, she appears as a spirit that dances in memoriam on the site of mass deaths, and in yet others she is herself a banshee and a death omen. While often the stories speak of a white lady, in Wales the stories become specific: the Lady Wyn is a specific Lady in White associated with Samhain. A white lady, on the other hand, can refer to a specific class of spirits mainly notable for appearing wearing white, usually in traditional funeral shrouds (Beck, 292–306).

Scholar J. C. Beck posits that White Lady/Lady Wyn lore is an example of the entity's gradual downgrade as Paganism waned and Christianity rose in Great Britain. The Lady Wyn may have begun as a goddess, then downgraded to a water/well spirit, and at last downgraded to a ghost story. A black sow, often associated with Lady Wyn, at one time symbolized the goddess Cerridwen in her crone aspect. This suggests that the Lady Wyn is actually the goddess Cerridwen, appearing to the inhabitants of the land in a new way (Cuhulain). As Christianity demonized Paganism in Europe, stories about her began to represent her as more wholly evil.

Along with the Black Pig, folk might encounter the Dullahan, or sometimes ghosts, not always of the friendly departed. The Black Pig, often associated with the White Lady, served as a diabolic image. Irish families often considered this pig an incarnation of the devil. In one Welsh ritual, when the bonfires went out, those tending it ran away shouting, "The cropped black sow seize the hindmost!" This tradition suggested running away from evil.

The Dullahan, sometimes described as a malicious imp, more often referred to a headless horseman that appeared on deserted roads at night. This personage appears as a death omen, carrying his own head at his side, and calling out the name of a person destined to die that night.

Another piece of lore involving horsemen as hunters, the Faery Host, bore a strong resemblance to Northern Europe's Wild Hunt. According to the Celtic lore, on Samhain night, the faery mounds opened and the Wild Host/Hunt (or Faery Host) came forth. Often this involved a hunting party, usually royal, accompanied by baying dogs, usually black, that ran ahead of and alongside the hunters. Some travelers might report seeing mortal adults kidnapped by this hunt—those who witnessed this often reported seeing their neighbors running with or from the Wild Hunt. The only way to avoid the hunt if caught outdoors was for the traveler to throw him or herself on the nearest soil, or better yet, into the nearest fallow field.

The identity of the hunters and their quarry changed according to the folklore of a given region. Sometimes the hunters came from other tales, such as King Arthur or King Herod; on other occasions locals identified the hunter as a man sinful or sacrilegious in life. Those hunted might also be recently departed community sinners, sometimes a lady in white, and sometimes woodland spirits. The Scottish added to this legend's atmosphere with tales of unbaptized infants wandering the woods at night, moaning.

In Northern Europe, people attributed the hunts to the gods of weather as well as the gods of death (in the case of Woden, these were one and the same.) Also called the Furious Host, locals believed that Odin himself led these hunts, sometimes accompanied by the goddesses Bertha and Holda. In addition to Odin's hunt, stories of the Goddess Bertha collecting troops of unbaptized children and flying them across the winter sky colored tales of the ghostly storm.

In attempts to explain what prompted the legends of the Wild Hunt, scholars looked to natural phenomena for explanations. As storm gods, Odin/Woden represented natural phenomena and storms, especially storms common just before winter. Some scholars thought that early Pagans interpreted thunder and howling storms as the Wild Hunt breaking into this world and giving chase to its prey. Another theory is that geese migrating across Great Britain and Europe in late October sounded like baying hounds at night. Yet another theory is that the wind in the trees prompted earlier people to think a hunt was afoot.

In yet another incarnation of this legend, sometimes it was just one hunter—the Specter Huntsman. Often this was a single hunter on horseback accompanied by dogs. The ghostly hunter often resembled either the Wild Hunt or the Dullahan.

The dogs/hounds that ran on these hunts also had their own flavor of lore. Nicknamed "Gabble Ratchets" or formally called Gabriel Ratchets, they were named after the Archangel Gabriel, who was believed to make announcements/deliver messages at the command of God. The sound or sight of these dogs, considered portentous, usually signaled death

for any lone traveler exposed to them. Some legends identified the dogs themselves as the souls of unbaptized children
or as will-o'-the-wisps (lights that hovered between heaven and
earth) that acted as spirits attempting to lure night travelers
to their deaths. These stories caused some people to avoid the
outdoors at Halloween, believing that seeing any apparition
could induce death.

Not all the fearsome things stayed outdoors, however. People took great care to prevent faeries from absconding with
human children or livestock on Samhain night. Cradles and
animals received a sprinkling with holy water or parents might
hang a parshell, a special type of cross, above the child's bed.
Parents placed a dead ember from the fire or iron in an infant's
cradle. Older children might have oatmeal or salt placed on
their heads. In addition, some families put food outside for the
faeries, in hopes of deterring them from helping themselves
to other living creatures around the property. The Irish had
a remedy for confrontation by faeries or malevolent spirits
on Halloween night: should one confront you on a darkened
road, throw some dust from under your feet at it. Then, run.

Trick-or-Treating

Trick-or-treating is a modern incarnation of old Irish, Manx,
and Scottish practices that sometimes occurred over multiple
nights leading to Samhain. In Ireland, the poor went door-to-

door "mumming" or "souling." They offered songs and prayers for the dead. As payment, the owners of the homes visited gave them soul cakes, cookies with a cross drawn on top, representing each soul detained in purgatory. Some saw the soulers, who often carried turnip lamps as they went about their rounds, as enacting the role of the dead souls seeking their food offerings. The regions that called this practice "mumming" were also referring to a type of folk theater called "Mummer's Theater." These often involved loose, strange plots involving stock characters. *Saint George and the Doctor* was a common play used at Samhain.

In Somerset, children went door-to-door on October 30, called "Punkie Night." The colloquial name "punkie" referred to their turnip (or beet) lanterns. On this holiday, children begged their neighbors for money to pay for fireworks used on the next night, called Mischief Night. The locals considered it unlucky to refuse—the children carrying the punkies represented the souls of dead children.

Some regions came to call this door-to-door collections practice *Halloween rhyming*. Often children sang a song to the people who answered their doors and soul cakes or soul meat was part of an expected exchange. Mumming in Ireland gave way to going door-to-door, saying, "Help the Halloween party! Any apples or nuts?"

In France, the tradition differed slightly. Rather than demanding food, children collected flowers from their neighbors, so that they might decorate graves of family members the following morning.

Pranks

As strange as it may sound, the Halloween tradition of pranks —even the obnoxious ones—has a foundation in Pagan tradition: blaming the faeries. While nothing on record speaks specifically to the logic or ritual of it, it seems that part of the holiday involved acting out a series of pranks either as a way of fooling the faeries or just because people might just blame the faeries, allowing the culprits to avoid consequences for the things they wanted to do. Many of the more popular pranks were "threshold" pranks, such as taking doors off hinges, soaping windows, and de-picketing fences.

Since the season marked a time of passage between the physical world and the spiritual, it's possible these pranks represented the breaking of the veil barriers. While any ritual intent has long since disappeared from record, spoken word records mention that often the recipients of these pranks were unpopular members of the community.

In Scotland, people call October 30 "Cabbage Night," and those in Nova Scotia call the same tradition "Cabbage Stump Night." To celebrate, spiteful people throw cabbage stumps at the doors of people they dislike. Perhaps this practice releases some anger in a manner that does less property damage than other expressions might cause.

In Scotland, when a father had daughters of marriageable age that he refused to let court, frustrated young men might wrap themselves in straw and break into the house of their would-be sweethearts, stuffing the girls' father up the chimney or stealing food and demanding a dance from the daughter.

In northern England, "Mischief Night" was a nickname for Halloween or for October 30. Typically a night of mayhem, young men threw fireworks in mailboxes, whitewashed windows, filled locks with glue, and stole gates. In Oxfordshire, people rolled tar barrels down the streets. In the North of England, teams pushed the tar barrels up and down streets in races. Many of the pranks played imitated the tricks attributed to faeries and goblins.

The pranks themselves often had traditional names and practices. For instance, in some areas of the United Kingdom and Canada, on October 31 it's common to rub chalk on someone's back, yell "Halloween!", and take off running. This practice, called chalking, may have originated from an obscure old holiday called Chalk-Back Day.

The Scottish prank called "Burning the Reekie Mehr" required a kale stalk filled with tallow. The prankster lit one end, put it against the keyhole of a victim's house, and blew on the other end until the house filled with smoke. Sometimes, when young women went to pull kale stalks, young men might leave a punkie out in the middle of the kale field to spook them.

While it's not known what spiritual role such mischief played on Allhallows (except, perhaps, to convince the goblins their services weren't needed) not only have the pranks continued and evolved, they are the main reason almost every city in the United States now allows trick-or-treating.

Costumes

What began with the Druids and ancient Celtic villagers dressing as animals or as frightening creatures such as ghosts and wandering the edge of their settlements in groups evolved into the moving ritual theater known as mumming. Along with singing traditional songs, sometimes those who performed also took on traditional costumes.

In South Wales, men and boys would dress as women while singing of a White Lady who sat in a tree accompanied by pigs and apples. Locals referred to these costumed characters as *gwarchod*, which translates to "hags." They often costumed themselves in sheepskin and wore ragged clothing and masks. In some areas, a man dressed as a horse accompanied mummers on their rounds. This character carried a horse skull painted black and decorated with ribbons, which he kept hidden under a white cloth. This traditionally had a jaw that snapped. This skull had several nicknames, such as "Old Hob" and "Wild Horse."

When the Irish came to the new world, they brought their costume traditions along. In colonial America, they had masquerade parades that over time caught on among their neighbors. The Victorian aesthetic popular in the United Kingdom and in the United States made Halloween a night much more tame than the folklore in its roots. Examples of this are apparent in vintage Halloween cards, showing young women participating in witchlike pursuits that refer to divination and other archaic practices in a way that suggests such games were trendy.

The costumes veered away from that of goblins, ghosts, and faeries in the 1930s when commercial costume companies appeared. The earliest costumes included characters relevant to that time—Little Orphan Annie, Mickey Mouse, and the ever-popular witch.

Parties and Games

Over the years, Halloween night became an evening to entertain children while adults reflected on the year prior and made plans for the year to come. These parties served as small family reunions, but also played a role in matchmaking, giving the eligible men and women of the community a chance to socialize. Apples, nuts, and kale all figured significantly into

Halloween/Samhain tradition, with the apples and nuts often given as gifts to children. This happened in part because kale came to maturity latest in the fall, and the winter stores of apples and nuts opened up around Samhain. A common nickname for Halloween was Nutcrack Night, in part because on that night people began eating the nuts collected earlier in the season.

Attendees played several games throughout the evening. The more popularly remembered games and superstitions involved apples. The United States and the United Kingdom had apple bobbing (also called apple ducking) as a common Hallowe'en game, where children attempted to remove apples from a tub of water with only their teeth. In the United Kingdom, a hostess might toss a silver coin to the bottom of the tub. The first to catch it hands-free kept the prize and was thought to be the first to marry. In colonial America, the first young woman to snag an apple won the title of the first to marry.

Another game played throughout the United Kingdom called Snap Apple dated back to the original Druids. In its initial form, the host tied an apple to one end of a rope, threw it across a barn rafter, and then tied a lit candle to the other end. Players had to catch the apple in his or her teeth without getting burned by the candle. This game gave way to a less dangerous form, still called Snap Apple (or in the United States sometimes "tethered apple") where the players tied apples to strings, suspended them from the ceiling (usually by tying the string around a rafter), and then swung them at one another tether-ball style while attempting to catch an apple with only the teeth. Those who won, according to divination, would have successful marriages within the year.

In addition to these games, apple peels and seeds had their own divination traditions. A person seeking information on a future spouse would peel an apple in a continuous spiral and throw it over his or her shoulder. The peel formed the first letter of the true love's first name. In one variation, the peel staying whole meant that the querent faced marriage by the end of the year, while the peel breaking meant the querent faced another year unwed. Women could take two seeds from the apple and place them on the cheek or eyelids after naming each after two opposite states of fortune—for example, wealth or poverty, travel or home, or marriage or spinsterhood. The first to fall off was the answer to the question. Cutting an apple in half, crossways, so that the center formed a star, might also serve as a divination tool. If two seeds appeared, the apple predicted an early marriage; three meant wealth or inheritance; four meant travel; five meant good health or a sea voyage; six meant wisdom or fame; and seven meant fame or a wish granted. Three guests might also hang apples on a string and stand in front of the fire; the first to have their apple fall would marry first, the last might never marry.

The abundance of nuts also led to their frequent use in Samhain and Autumn Equinox divinations. A favorite method determined the compatibility of a couple. If two nuts, named after a pair of lovers and thrown in a fire burned bright together, it foretold a happy marriage. Two nuts jumping apart warned of arguments. A nut failing to ignite meant the pair faced unhappiness.

Cabbage and kale also configured into popular divination and Halloween magickal practices. The most practiced of these involved young men and women old enough to marry sneaking into a kale patch at midnight and pulling up a stalk without looking at it. The youngest person hung the kale above the bedroom door overnight and then examined it the next day. The character of the kale purportedly revealed the character of the kale thief's future spouse. For instance, a plant with lots of soil meant marrying rich. One with a black core meant the future spouse had a temper. Longer plants meant a tall sweetheart.

One party game called for naming seven kale stalks after seven people present. The partygoers pulled the stalk, and then each person witnessed an examination of their own character through kale. If the person that pulled the kale hung it over a door on Halloween night, the first person to walk beneath it the next day could take it, place it beneath his or her pillow, and have an excellent dream about the future. Children in want of a new brother or sister would pile kale outside their parents' door in hopes that it might result in a sibling.

Many of the Samhain divination traditions revolved around the identity of the future spouse, especially as November was the month that the most weddings occurred. In the alphabet game, a diviner cut every letter of the alphabet from a newspaper and then floated the letters in a bowl of water. The letters that floated to the top could reveal the name of a future spouse. In a similar game, young men were encouraged to write the names of female friends on slips of paper and then wrap the papers in dough. The young men then cast the dough onto the water: the woman revealed when the dough melted away was the young man's true love. If perhaps he had trouble making decisions, someone wrote three names in the dust of a fireplace mantle and the one the young man's finger landed on revealed his true love.

In another scenario, a young woman might, on Halloween day, go and thresh wheat, believing she would have a vision of her future mate by the time she finished her work. In a less strenuous version, a curious person might climb to some point that no four-footed animal could (usually a house roof) and close his or her eyes. The first animal spotted upon opening the eyes indicated characteristics of the future spouse. In an equally accident-prone variation, a person shut his or her eyes and walked backward to the end of his or her house. Upon opening the eyes, the first thing seen indicates the nature of fortune in the coming year. Among the things that were lucky to see were men, especially men on horses. In this superstition, seeing a woman foretold ill luck, especially spying an old woman; seeing anyone digging or a bird with its head under its wing were also bad.

The fire and its ashes also held answers for Halloween truth seekers. Betrothed people were encouraged to blow on the ashes of a fire. If the ashes flew into the face, it warned of an unhappy marriage. The ashes around the hearth the morning after Halloween foretold the future—a footprint toward the front door meant a death within the year and one away from it meant marriage. In colonial North America, a blindfolded person would walk across a ring of fireplace ashes or flour. A footprint toward the door didn't mean death of a loved one: it just meant bad luck, and a footprint away from the door meant good luck or marriage within the year.

Several marriage divinations involved performing proscribed actions for calling that person's "fetch" or astral self from the body to the diviner's local for the sake of identification. For example, in one popular spell, a young woman sowed a row of hemp seed at midnight on Allhallows. As she sat and watched, the apparition of her husband to be would appear to furrow the seed. In another version, a young woman would hang her nightgown in front of the fire and then watch the room through the keyhole of the closed door, waiting to see the ghost of her future husband come and turn the garment. She might instead choose, on Hallowe'en, to sit in front of a mirror at midnight, eating an apple and combing her hair— the man destined for her would appear to her over her left shoulder.

In a sort of inversion of the dumb supper, a young woman might also seek to see her lover's form with "dumb cake" by mixing dough with any liquid except spring water. She would do this using her left thumb only, performing the kneading in total silence, and at midnight pricked her initials on them with a new pin before putting them into an oven to bake. She then sat on the opposite side of the room, waiting in silence for her the form of her future lover to appear and check on the cake's progress.

A young man might pull flowers from the horse-knot plant and cut the tops off the stamens, then hide the flower from view. If, on All Saint's morning, he found the stamens shot back to their original height, he knew his sweetheart returned his love.

In yet another variation, a woman would throw a blue ball of yarn out a window and chant the Lord's Prayer in reverse while rewrapping the yarn and gazing out the window looking for the ghostly figure of her future partner. The yarn ball divination sometimes took place with presumed faery participation. In one version, someone threw an entire string of unraveled blue yarn into a limekiln. This person then rewound it until he or she felt resistance from inside the kiln. If nothing tugged, the diviner might die unmarried.

In another version, an unwed miller might perform this divination with the help of brownies called *Killmovlis* that specialized in mills. While often these creatures appeared to live to annoy the miller, they also seemed protective of the mill itself and sometimes did help with the work. At midnight on Halloween, the miller, seeking the name of his future wife, threw the ball of yarn in a kiln and again rewrapped until he felt resistance. The miller assumed the tension came from a Killmovli taking hold of the other end of the yarn inside the kiln. The miller would call "what holds?" and the brownie would, from his hiding space, snort the name of the future spouse.

While most Samhain divination games revolved around marriage questions, people also brought their concerns about health, career, weather, and wealth to the party. Farmers watched their bull to see what way it lay down on Hallowe'en—the direction indicated the direction of most wind through the winter. If Samhain fell on a Wednesday, farmers expected a rough winter. People threw shoes over houses to determine where they might be in the coming year: whatever direction they pointed indicated the direction that thrower might travel. There were multiple "three plates" divinations, where each plate contained something symbolizing a future possibility. Often mothers entertained children by piercing an egg, dropping the egg white into the glass of water, and foretelling future based on the visions created by the swirling white.

Despite the best efforts of the ninth century Christian Church, Samhain did not so much return as it remained. That, alongside Halloween, speaks to humanity's enduring need to acknowledge fear, death, uncertainty, and loss. Samhain offers a chance for renewal and a chance to connect lovingly with the dead again. Halloween offers a release from the norm—often exactly what people need after enduring powerful grief. Pagans celebrate life, and with Samhain they do so by revering the dead, celebrating the chain of lives that brought us all together.

NEW WAYS

carnelian, wisdom, surviṿal, preservation, hunting, other worlds,

ling, release from old bonds, road openings, fire, protection su

s of scorpio, sun sign of scorpio, dark moon, pleiades at highe

at midnight, the crone, the grieving mother, the grieving wife,

eter, Persephone and Hades, Ereshkigal, Osiris, Janus, Cer

rnunnos, the Daghda, Hecate, Dis Pater, Hel, Inanna, I

e, Lilith, Macha, Mare, the Morrigan, Osiris, Isis, I

Rhiannon, Samana, Teutates, Taranis, the Horned God, th

orange-brown, yellow, grey, green, cedar, dittany of crete, sag

corn, wheat, rye, pumpkins, hazel, hemlock, chrysanthemum, ca

arigold, jet, obsidian, onyx, carnelian, moonstone, iron, black a

rs, owls, ravens, decaying leaves, myrrh, copal, death, wheel of

igh priestess, cauldron, mask, besom, apple, pumpkin, fermented

kraut, pickled eggs, pickled beets, roasted nuts, raw nuts, apple

wood, divination, soul cakes, sugar skulls, jack-o-lanterns, ta

bobbing, seances, scrying, bonfires, trick-or-treating, mummer

in off gravesites, dedicate memorials, visit nursing homes, sam

calan gaef, calan gaef, gealach a ruadhain, calan gaef, kalo

$\mathcal{M}$ANY PAGANS CELEBRATE modern Samhain on October 31, the same day as Halloween. Some, however, prefer to perform their observances on the full moon closest to the sabbat date. Others consult almanacs to determine the official astrological cross-quarter day.

Often it is a quiet, solemn occasion in private Pagan households. Many see it as the most important ritual of the year. Families with small children will often negotiate a compromise to let their children enjoy the costumes, pageantry, and candy while also honoring their own traditions.

Modern Themes and Common Elements

While Halloween has become almost entirely secular, Samhain has retained much of its spiritual flavor. It is still a day to honor the dead and to think about death along with other things that we fear. It is still a time to meditate and reflect, and people still perform divinations, enjoy feasts, and sometimes light bonfires during this holiday. While All Souls' Day has also changed in character over the centuries, the Pagan Samhain actually aligns with the Christian holiday in terms of spiritual intent.

In the City

Those who live in towns and cities can partake in the most famous Halloween tradition: trick-or-treating. Every year, usually during hours set by the municipality, parents or older siblings take costumed youngsters door-to-door to ask for candy. In return, the neighbors distributing candy get their very own costume pageant delivered to their door.

Along with this tradition comes a tradition many people do not enjoy—one of all night mischief and vandalism. While most of the time vandals stick to smashing jack-o'-lanterns and throwing toilet paper in trees, some do more damage than that. This goes back to old Irish traditions where mischief makers would pull pickets off fences, takes doors off hinges, or even break windows. These practices were closely associated with threshold magick—not that it made the tradition any less frustrating for the person stuck repairing the mess the next day!

In the Country

People who celebrate Samhain or Halloween in rural areas often partake in slightly different traditions. In some areas, houses are too sparse for trick-or-treating to be practical for families with children. Often in those situations, community members gather in public schools or community buildings and host a communal Halloween party. Along with treats, children get to play games such as apple bobbing or balloon darts, and adults and teenagers can enjoy a scary movie in a different room. If a community is so sparse that this is not possible, Pagans often turn their focus toward the family practices that they themselves have established for the season.

A Few Halloween/Samhain Myths Debunked

As the years go on, historians and archaeologists often turn up information that proves old information wrong. One such example is the case of Pomona's Day. While many sources popularly attribute Pomona's Day to October 31, an investigation of the ancient Roman calendar reveals that any celebration of her or of an orchard harvest happened August 23 and did not have any direct association with death or ancestral themes.

One theory about how this association came to be is that when Christianity overtook the Celtic Isles, the military government often moved the days of locally celebrated holidays to different times of year as a means of reducing their influence. According to this theory, when the Romans invaded Celtic lands, the church decided to combine Pomona's observances with the Celtic Pagan death observances. Over time, people came to assume that these holidays coincided.

In the modern age, such misinformation is not yet historical inaccuracy but is instead urban legend. For instance, in the 1970s, concerned parents became fearful that their neighbors might stick razor blades or poisons in the candy given out to trick-or-treaters. Hospitals and police stations began to offer to x-ray candy hauls, and it eliminated the distribution of homemade candies or natural fruits such as apples. There was never a single reported instance of a child finding a razor blade or worse in his or her candy bag, but the fear won out, and the tradition of homemade edible treats disappeared.

Different Pagans, Different Practices

Many modern Pagans celebrate Samhain, either on the full moon closest to October 31 or on that date itself. While Celtic in origin, Pagans may celebrate in a way culturally appropriate to their tradition. At Samhain season, it is appropriate to invoke the Morrighan, Dagda, Hades, Persephone, Hecate, and many other death and Witchcraft deities across many pantheons. For those who practice quieter, home-based traditions this is often a time of dumb suppers, quiet divination, and family reflection. The list of traditions mentioned here is far from exhaustive—many Pagans may also observe feasts dedicated to specific chthonic deities through the month of November in addition to or in place of Samhain.

Wicca

Wiccans consider Samhain the end of the old year and the beginning of the new. At this point in the sabbat cycle, the Goddess has descended from the earth to the land of the dead, where she will see and mate with her beloved, the dying god. Her opening the door to the world of the dead is believed to be why the veil thins, and there are rituals practiced to honor her descent and to honor the dead, especially those who died in the year prior.

Celtic Wiccans follow the Wiccan Rede and the God/Goddess soft duotheism but also believe in and work with the Celtic pantheon. Celtic Wiccans celebrate Samhain with common Wiccan rituals, including ancestor altars, dumb suppers, and divination. They often invoke Celtic gods and goddesses of death or those directly associated with Samhain such as the Morrighan.

Celtic Reconstruction

Celtic Reconstructionists are Pagans who are trying to rebuild ancient Celtic Paganism as exactly as possible. They call Samhain *Oiche Shamnhna,* and try to make their observations as close to the first frost as possible (NicDhana). Often the Morrighan is venerated at this time. In Irish myth, Samhain marks the day that she and the Tuatha de Danaan god Dagda mated at the River Unis.

In this myth, the Morrighan represents the forces of death and the moon, while the Dagda represents the sun and life. In addition to honoring this lore, Celtic Reconstructionists may smudge their homes with juniper, establish an altar to honor the dead, and prepare a feast with the first foods set on a plate at a reserved seat at the table or at the altar for the dead. At this dinner, people share memories of their departed loved ones and make toasts. After the meal, there is divination and storytelling.

Druidry

For Druids, October 31 is Samhain—a festival to honor the dead. They have many names for it, often based on their own Celtic cultural alignment. Names include *La Samhna*, *Sauin*, or *Souney* (November). Some also call it *Calan Gaeaf*, *Calan Gwaf* (first day of winter), or *Nos Cyn Calan Gual* (first night of winter), among many other names. It was one of the four fire festivals. In their spiritual tradition the *Cailleach* (Crone) comes to strip the leaves from the trees, and because of the veil thinning, all time becomes one time: past, present, and future happen simultaneously on Samhain night. This synchronization makes it possible for the dead to walk among the living and for the living to communicate with their dead. Often the modern observance will include a bonfire along with a remembrance of the dead.

Traditional Witchcraft

Traditional witches of Britain see Samhain as one of the great four fire festivals. Samhain is one of three nights of the year when the veil between worlds grows thin (the other two being May Eve and Midsummer). Some traditional witches cast two circles during their Samhain ceremonies—one for the living and one for the dead. It is a time of communing with the dead, especially ancestors, and traditional witches may make it a point to visit a cemetery, crossroad, or burial mound at this time. Samhain is considered a time to connect to the dark God and Goddess and to meditate on what they have to teach.

Eclectic Witchcraft

Eclectic witches borrow from different traditions in a manner that spiritually resonates with them. During Samhain, they often celebrate by honoring their physical ancestors but also their spiritual ancestors, including other witches and Pagans from before their time. Rituals focus on the dark of the year and often invoke gods of the dead from different pantheons. Persephone and Pluto, Kali Ma, the Morrighan and the Dagda, and the Norse goddess Hel are all possibilities during an eclectic Samhain ritual.

Neopagan

Neopagans do not necessarily identify with any one tradition or method of practice, nor are they interested in going through the initiatory practices common to Wicca and some forms of Witchcraft. For those who celebrate Samhain, it is a time to set out ancestor altars, to tell stories about people who have gone before us, to practice divination, and to gather around bonfires or attend public Samhain rituals and share in a sense of spiritual community.

Stregheria

Practitioners of Stregha, an Italian-rooted Witchcraft, call October 31 *La Festa del Ombra*, or Shadowfest. At this time, the goddess of their pantheon descends to the underworld to confront death. There, she meets the god Dis, and a dialogue about why things must suffer and die ensues. While she is there, they have intercourse and there is a sharing of mysteries. Streghas set out meals for spirits, leave milk and honey for faery folk, and remember their beloved dead.

Heathen

Norse (or Asatru) Pagans call October 31 the Winternights. Some may call this date Elf-Finding or Frey finding. At this time, they honor ancestors, give thanks for the land, and honor both death and all wisdom. The ancestral Norse considered this date summer's end. On October 31, someone fells the last sheaf of the harvest, then blesses it and leaves it in the field. From this night on, they believe that the Wild Hunt—a ghostly party that hunts any traveler it might catch— rules the night.

Hellenic Pagans

Hellenic Pagans do not align with the Celtic pantheon. Instead, they spend the month of October honoring Aries and the month of November honoring Artemis. Boedromion (roughly September–October) does have a festival of the dead called Genesia that mainly honors deceased parents. Since the exact process of celebration is unclear in historical sources, Hellenic Reconstructionists make private choices whether to observe the holiday. A few may make a personal choice to align the celebration with Samhain as a matter of community connection, but Celtic holidays fall outside Hellenic practices.

Feri Witchcraft

Those who practice the Feri tradition of Witchcraft believe in ecstatic union with the divine. This means that rituals involve direct engagement through dancing, chanting, and trance work. At Samhain, they perform a ritual where they open a gate to the land of the dead, and through that gate call to deities to come and prepare them for death. They spend most of their Samhain rituals communing with their departed loved ones.

Reclaiming

Witches who practice the Reclaiming Tradition consider themselves to be reclaiming the powers of equality and justice. In San Francisco, every Samhain they honor the holiday, and their justice work with a large, public spiral dance. In this dance, people join hands and dance in a grapevine step together. From an aerial view, the movement forms a giant spiral.

In Wicca and other initiatory Pagan traditions, Samhain is also a popular time for initiations and degree elevations. Often the initiations are part of the Samhain ceremonies or take place in the weeks after Samhain, filling up the ritual calendar for covens between Samhain and Yule. Because most Pagans consider initiation profoundly transformational, they see the thinned veil as the optimal time for dramatic change—the old self (preinitiated) dies to the world and the newly initiated takes that former person's place.

Other Holidays and Practices

While Samhain and Halloween are the best-known holidays at this time of year, there are others. Many are festivals of the dead or preparations for winter.

All Souls' Day, also called All Saints' Day

All Souls' Day happens on November 1 or on the first Sunday of November depending on the Christian denomination. Originally part of the Christian attempt to absorb Samhain and similar festivals of the dead, it became an observance intertwined with the Pagan holidays that honor the dead. This day of holy obligation in the Catholic Church is a time to pray for all the dead and to ask for the intercession of the dead that ascended to heaven. In Catholic tradition, these prayers were necessary because of a belief that certain souls remained in purgatory, an afterlife halfway between heaven and hell, where souls might work out their issues before moving on.

Catholic and Orthodox Christians observe these holidays with the most ceremony. Some denominations split the observances into two holidays, with November 1 as All Saints' Day and November 2 as All Souls' Day. November 2 is for the souls that might still have some sin to work off in purgatory. Whether or not these dead need the prayers of the living is a point of controversy among some Christians.

Dia de los Muertos

In Mexico, the holiday *Dia de Los Muertos* on November 1, honors the dead with food, processions, and flowers. The practice of honoring the dead had been part of Aztec life long before the Conquistadores arrived. However, the arrival of the Catholic Church in Mexico meant subjection to a Catholic routine. Rather than ban the day, the church overwrote its meaning with All Souls' Day and moved the date from roughly July or August to November 1. Instead of supplanting the day of the dead practices, this move by the Catholic Church sanctified the holiday for the people observing it.

During the season, people build altars to their departed loves ones, make skulls out of wood and candy, clean and decorate graves, and hold picnics at the gravesite of dead loved ones. It is different from All Souls' Day in that those who observe it welcome the possibility of visitations in their homes from their ancestors.

Autumn Dziady

In Slavic countries, October 31 to November 2 are also days of festivals of the dead. Those who practice Christianity go to cemeteries of their departed relatives on November 1 and light candles, so their loved ones may find their way to heaven or to home. Those who practice old Pagan traditions (or sometimes practice both the old Pagan and the modern Christian traditions) also host what the Scotts and Irish called a dumb supper on November 2. The Slavs call this a *Dziady*. They set out a place at their dinner tables, complete with extra spoons, and the family speaks in whispers telling stories of their departed loved ones. They believe that any manifestation of nature during the dinner, from a breeze to an insect, represents an ancestral visitation.

These ancestor dinners are practiced three or four times a year, with specific seasonal rituals related to each one. The Slavic people who still practice this live mainly in Eastern Poland, Lithuania, and Belarus. Polish poet Adam Mickiewicz wrote a play about this folk practice, including scenes where villagers brought food and drink to abandoned houses and then counseled the dead according to folk wisdom instead of according to the dominant Christian mores.

Hop-tu-Naa

The Isle of Man still celebrates Hop-tu-Naa, a sort of ancestor to modern Halloween and descendant of the original Samhain. Considered an observance of the Celtic New Year, called *"Oie Houney"* by the Manx, on October 31 children go door to door carrying lanterns carved of turnips and singing. Hop-tu-Naa mummers sing traditional songs in Gaelic, such as one that translates to "This is Old Hollantide night / the moon shines bright." In turn, the neighbors distribute coins—in modern days for UNICEF but sometimes even now for fireworks to set off sometime between October 31 and November 5.

Mischief Night / Guy Fawkes Day

The Great Britain bonfires of October 31 eventually moved to November 5. While some areas refer to this time as Mischief Night, the Catholic Church / Church of England eventually called it Guy Fawkes Day, after a man named Guy Fawkes, who was arrested when discovered underneath the House of Parliament guarding explosives intended to blow up the building. On this day, younger people set off fireworks and ring bells, ostensibly for the health and safety of the queen and parliament while burning effigies of Guy Fawkes. While meant as a warning against treason, the release of the movie *V for Vendetta* subverted the meaning of the Guy Fawkes mask into a symbol of just rebellion. Guy Fawkes Day replaced the original Mischief Night and for the most part replaced the traditional bonfires of Samhain night in the United Kingdom.

Modern Samhain Gatherings and Festivals

While not all modern Pagans necessarily celebrate Samhain, or celebrate Samhain on October 31, they often find reasons to come together at the end of October and the beginning of November. Many Pagan organizations choose to start and stop their annual calendar around this date. Often Pagans consider the "holiday" season that encompasses Thanksgiving and Christmas to begin with Samhain.

Public Rituals

Sometimes local covens or larger Pagan organizations hold public rituals at Samhain. These rituals may be small or large, indoors or outdoors. They often take place a few days before October 31 to accommodate those who also have private celebrations on that date. Covenant of the Goddess and Reclaiming tradition both have well-known annual public Samhain rituals. You can often find listings of these events in local Pagan shops, online at the Witch's Voice, and sometimes via Meetup.com.

Witches' Balls

When in a position to do so, Pagan communities throughout the United States will hold a witches' ball near Samhain but not on it, so as not to conflict with private Samhain celebrations. These celebrations often include food, drink, dancing, music, and of course costumes! People looking for events to attend can check the Witch's Voice website for special Samhain events around the United States. Well known witches' balls have happened in New Orleans, Denver, Detroit, and Salem. If you do not have one in your area, start one! Large gathering events take about a year to plan, so use your Samhain meditation time to figure out how best to go about starting the event, and work some magick for the right people to help you to come your way.

Secular Gatherings and Festivals

While Samhain, like *Dia de los Muertos*, is still very much a religious festival, many Pagans blend their sacred home traditions with some of the celebratory aspects of the sacred holiday. Often this includes participating in the fun events of the season: horror movie marathons, masquerades, hayrides, and visiting haunted houses!

Haunted Houses

Every Halloween season also comes with fun events leading up to Halloween. One of the more popular activities is the haunted house. In this experiential theater, the audience walks through a darkened building and faces frightening or silly scenes. The people who create them range from people fundraising for charities to artists wanting a new interactive medium to entertainment companies seeking profit from the billions that Halloween generates every year. Locations for haunted houses can be almost anything. They have been set in private homes, churches, old warehouses, shut down jails, and barns. Some farmers have even enhanced their traditional hayrides with haunted walks in the woods and monstrous scenery as the tractor pulls its passengers past.

Costume Parties

The tradition of dressing as the frightening things of the night has given way to dressing as whatever might strike your fancy. For children, costumes are part of the exchange of trick-or-treating. For adults, they are a way to have fun sanctioned only at Halloween or science fiction conventions. Often people dress for masquerade parties where a costume is required for admission. Because of the convention-breaking nature of the holiday, people also often wear costumes to work or while going about errands on Halloween day. For Pagans, wearing a costume is a matter of personal taste. Many participate in this fun, while others choose not to because they already wear robes and other specific ritual clothing during their actual ceremonies.

Trick-or-Treating

What was once the poor going to wealthy houses and seeking soul cakes in exchange for prayers transformed in the New World to small children approaching their neighbors with the call "trick-or-treat!" The neighbors get the entertainment of seeing cute children in small costumes, and those who are not parents often get to hand sugar to children they do not have to look after later. The ritual call "trick-or-treat" is not the genuine threat it once was. It used to be that if a neighbor—likely citing religious objections—refused to provide a treat to the children wandering door-to-door, a trick indeed would follow.

The history of threshold tricks (removing pickets from fences or taking doors off hinges) gave way to smashed jack-o'-lanterns, eggs thrown at houses, toilet paper in yards, and broad ranging pranks that run the border between vandalism and performance art. Ordinances regulating the ages of trick-or-treaters vary from city to city, but often these do help preserve the public fun in Halloween while minimizing the property damage. Nowadays most people consider trick-or-treating a ritual formality rather than a genuine threat.

Many Pagans genuinely enjoy trick-or-treaters. Cute kids in costumes are always fun, and many Pagans have children themselves, so they also participate! Most of the time, trick-or-treating happens before sunset so that there isn't too much of a problem. Sometimes, however, when Pagans are practicing their own Samhain observations they may need a quiet, uninterrupted time to observe. The custom, when this happens, is to leave the porch light off. Most trick-or-treaters respect the policy.

Treats Instead of Candy

While we think of "treat" as something to eat these days, a treat is any small thing that induces a sense of pleasure. To children, a toy, a story, or a new experience is as much of a treat as sugar. If you prefer to give something besides candy, consider one of these do-it-yourself approaches to satisfy trick-or-treaters.

Small story scrolls: Print tiny stories about Halloween onto a sheet of paper, cut them into tiny sheets, roll up the scrolls and tie them with a ribbon. If you have children, ask them to make up their own three or four line stories to go on the scrolls.

Origami fortune cookies: Honor the tradition of Samhain divination without adding to the pile of sugar! Make paper fortune cookies out of origami paper or out of square-cut magazine paper and insert fun fortunes or silly facts on small sheets of paper that you insert inside the "cookie."

Miniature cootie-catchers: Honor the Samhain tradition of divination with this middle school origami trick. Called cootie-catchers or paper fortunetellers, you can write down numbers, symbols, or names on the inside. These are simple to make but can take some time. These make a good project during a scary movie marathon.

Cootie-catcher

Homemade rainbow crayons: If your family uses crayons heavily, you probably have a collection of crayon stubs too small for use but too large to discard. Give them new life by making rainbow crayons. Gather the crayon stubs in a silicon mold of any shape you like—if you can get a Halloween-themed mold, even better! Place the mold on a cookie sheet and place in your oven at its lowest setting. Leave for thirty minutes. Turn off the heat, and remove the sheet and mold. Allow to cool. When finished, you can pop the crayons out of the mold and you now have a rainbow crayon to give out to your trick-or-treaters!

Give a book: In 2010, renowned fantasy and comic writer Neil Gaiman made a proposal: give away books for Halloween. You can gather books at garage and library sales, or gather stacks of books you know you won't re-read. If you have a lot of thrift stores in your area, talk to the managers about buying out the children's books in bulk—you can often get a discount for taking inventory off their hands.

Suggested Activities

Halloween/Samhain has a host of fun activities for adults or children. Fill the month of October with all sorts of spooky decor, service activities, or divination games.

Pumpkin Carving

For older children and adults, pumpkin carving is still a messy but beloved Samhain tradition. If you can, carve pumpkins in an outdoor space, but if the weather does not permit, make sure to spread newspaper all over the working area—including areas you think couldn't possibly get pumpkin on them. It's possible, especially with children present.

If you want to tap into history and have more advanced carving skills, also buy some beets and turnips and carve those. You will have to work smaller and, unlike pumpkins, they are not as soft on the inside, so scooping them out takes much more work.

When done, many people place tea lights inside. However, autumn winds do not always cooperate, so many people put LED lights and flashlights inside. If you are feeling especially playful, put a noise-making motion sensor toy inside—it will alert you if someone has wicked designs upon your helpless pumpkin!

Bonfires

A bonfire goes back to the days of the Druids when the surrounding villagers doused their hearth fires and then lit them from a flame carried from the Samhain fire. While modern power companies have made this tradition moot, the bonfire still aligns with those old rites. Try having a formal ceremony where you light a candle from the fire that you then bring into your house. You may also want to practice scrying by gazing at the bottom of the flames, observing what visions flash within your mind.

Fun with Apples

Apples configured into harvest celebrations from September through November. Associated with the wicked witches that are everywhere during Samhain season, apple games flavor the season.

Apple Peel Divination: While this used to determine the initial of who a young man or woman might marry, these days lengthened life spans and less economic need for marriage has transformed it. So should you take a vegetable peeler or paring knife and strip an apple of its skin in one long slice and throw the peel over your shoulder, assume that the letters it forms are the initials of your next romantic partner, whether or not you end up married.

Apples on a String: If you set up a bonfire, try playing this divination game: tie one string each to three apples. Have three people stand before the fire, each one with an apple held before the fire by its string. The first apple to fall belongs to the one who will marry first. If an apple clings to its string until the fire dies down, that person will never marry.

Snap Apple: This works best in a space that has rafters or open pipes. Suspend apples from the rafters with a string or tie the apples to a pole that can reach the ceiling. Have a contest to see who can get a bite from the apple while keeping his or her hands behind his or her back.

Bobbing for Apples: Save this game for adults and older teens—this might lead to some safety issues (or at least lost retainers) with the younger set! Float apples in a large tub of water. Again, players may not use their hands and may only remove the apples with their teeth. Sometimes the Scottish would throw a silver coin in the bottom of the tub, usually claimed by the lucky person with the best lung capacity. This game is usually more enjoyable for teenagers and adults than for younger children.

Make Your Own Haunted House

While visiting haunted houses is fun, working in one is even more fun! You may take a serious, scary, or silly approach to it: perhaps set up a three-dimensional walk through your favorite underworld and have the tour guides aspect those that guided the dead. You may also want to reenact favorite scenes from horror movies (or horror spoofs), or have people meet different dead celebrities along their path. Consider this if you are looking for a fundraiser for your current Pagan organization!

Adopt an Ancestor

Most communities have old cemeteries in them. Some still get loving maintenance while others languish in neglect. This decay especially happens in rural cemeteries. Host a solemn procession in a cemetery, in one that allows you to strew flowers. Go to a cemetery with a friend or two, or with your children, and look closely at the neglected gravesites. If it feels right to you, tend to that grave. Clean off any leaves or debris, call in any vandalism you happen to see to the cemetery keepers, and when done give a small offering of water to the soil of the grave. Before you leave, pause to address a prayer to the gods or the land, asking that this soul be restful and the grave be honored. This is a gentle way of honoring all ancestors, especially those time has forgotten.

Adopt a Living Ancestor

This is a good time of year to volunteer in nursing homes. Since this is a time of ancestral exploration, it's also a good time to talk to the strangers next door about their own history. The world has changed rapidly in the past century, especially in the ways we travel and share information. Spend some time interviewing those born before 1950 about how they used to celebrate Halloween, and if they didn't, ask what they did during autumn.

Create a Safer Halloween

If too many people in your community use Halloween as an excuse for bad behavior, make an effort to change that! Most police forces or sheriff's departments have a citizen-based volunteer core that can patrol the streets and keep an eye out for harmful behavior. You can also connect with someone who runs the neighborhood watch on your street.

Perhaps, however, you live in a community where the police run into misunderstandings with public Pagan rituals. Rather than repeating difficult cycles and hoping nothing will happen, be proactive! Offer yourself or your group as a resource to the police when they think a crime might involve the occult, and invite them to friendly question and answer sessions well before any public ritual. Be sure to inquire with your parks department or city hall about public ordinances that might concern your group if you are doing a public outdoor ritual. While this won't work in all areas—sometimes people's superstitions about religions other than their own will always outweigh the facts, but in many areas, the police appreciate proactive outreach.

Have a Divination Party

Samhain is the season for divination. Invite like-minded friends over to try out modern and historic methods of prognostication. Try reading for one another using tarot, runes, the *I Ching*, or even a Magic 8 Ball. If you feel adventurous, make a game of inventing a divination method. Perhaps serve an Irish divination based dessert: make a cake and bake in a ring, a thimble, and a coin. The ring means marriage, the thimble being single, and the coin riches.

If you can clean up your roof easily and you won't anger the landlord or the neighbors, try throwing shoes over your house. Wherever the shoe lands points the direction that the person who throws it will go in the next year. If you have practice reading tea leaves, try serving tea. Or perform the egg-white divination where you drop egg white from a pierced egg into a glass of water and read the shapes therein. Keep a bowl of hazelnuts available; if you have a bonfire going, guests can take two hazelnuts, name each one after a person and throw them into the fire—if they crackle and jump apart, these people are incompatible; if they jump closer, they'll get on just fine. Take turns with guests, having them hold water in their mouths and listening to the party outside of a window—the first names they hear in the eavesdropped conversation will be a name of significance to them in the coming year.

The Candle Chain

Druid traditions found ways to survive in new forms in historic Ireland. While lighting all hearth fires from the sacred Samhain fire disappeared into Christian tradition, the Irish found a clever way around it. As clergyman James Keller once said, "A candle loses nothing by lighting another candle." In October, Irish women set about making one candle to represent their household. The woman of the house would then light that candle and take it to her neighbor, offering prayers of blessing. The neighbor would then light a candle she made from that flame, which she in turn gave to the next neighbor. Soon each house stood connected, light by light, from the passing of the candle to each household.

Start a chain of candle prayers just like the old Irish. Ask a few magick-friendly friends to join you on this; if it goes well you can make it a running tradition. If you want to make candles, wonderful, but simply buying a bag of tea lights or votives of any color will do.

Tell Stories

Storytelling is how all spiritual traditions continue and grow. Samhain itself may have the richest soil of all for these stories. Every human being has some type of story in them, even if it's a small one. Tell a story about a grandparent—something that he or she taught you, something that he or she did that made you laugh, something that made you wonder about the mysteries of their lives, or the memories that they never shared with you. If you can spin a spooky yarn, do. Often people love to share tales of their personal spooky experiences, such as moments sighting ghosts or sensing the future. The most diverting evenings are the ones filled with stories shared.

Hold a Magickal Movies Marathon

One of the less verbalized themes of Samhain is one that horror and fantasy movies capture the best: magick is possible. Invite friends over who also love this genre and watch some movies or television shows that explore the themes of magick, life after death, bending veils in time, and alternate worlds. Some suggested titles you might want to try:

Dead Like Me
Wonderfalls
Practical Magick
Mirror Mask
What Dreams May Come
Haven
Midnight in Paris

Hold a Samhain Vigil

The Irish used to sit up with the hearth fire on Samhain night. If you don't have a fire to tend, you can still do something fire-related—make candles! Use this time to meditate on the year past and set intentions for the year ahead. You may have more success if you only choose one goal and spend the evening planning the small steps you need to take to achieve that single goal. If you prefer a quieter evening, keep yourself up with this crafty pursuit.

Samhain is a very serious holiday, just as Halloween is immensely fun. This does not cause conflict for most Pagans because celebration is often just as much a part of Pagan religions as reverence. Many Pagans are especially fond of both Halloween and Samhain—these holidays honor the dead and let us remember their fun and funny moments when alive. Halloween also encourages us to face our fears and to celebrate that magick is possible.

SPELLS
AND
DIVINATION

...en-... are ... courage, happiness, endings, cha-
rnation, wisdom, survival, preservation, hunting, other worlds,
...ing, release from old bonds, road openings, fire, protection sun
of scorpio, sun sign of scorpio, dark moon, pleiades at highes...
at midnight, the crone, the grieving mother, the grieving wife, t...
...ter, Persephone and Hades, Ereshkigal, Osiris, Janus, Cerr...
...nunos, the Daghda, Hecate, Dis Pater, Hel, Inanna, I...
..., Lilith, Macha, Mare, the Morrigan, Osiris, Isis, P...
Rhiannon, Samana, Teutates, Taranis, the Horned God, the...
orange-brown, yellow, grey, green, cedar, dittany of crete, sage...
...orn, wheat, rye, pumpkins, hazel, hemlock, chrysanthemum, cat...
...rigold, jet, obsidian, onyx, carnelian, moonstone, iron, black ca...
...s, owls, ravens, decaying leaves, myrrh, copal, death, wheel of ...
...h priestess, cauldron, mask, besom, apple, pumpkin, fermented ...
...raut, pickled eggs, pickled beets, roasted nuts, raw nuts, apple...
...wool, divination, soul cakes, sugar skulls, jack-o-lanterns, bo...
...bobbing, seances, scrying, bonfires, trick-or-treating, mummer's ...
...n off gravesites, dedicate memorials, visit nursing homes, samh...
...alan gaef, calan gaef, gealach a ruadhain, calan goef, hala-y...

$\mathcal{O}$CTOBER AND NOVEMBER are intensely magickal times of the year, in part because of their in-between states. It's not quite the end of fall, but it's definitely not winter yet (in the Northern Hemisphere) and that makes the world a spooky, changeable place. Magickal folks love that atmosphere—all the better for casting spells and throwing cards. After all, Samhain is when anything can happen, and magick is about ensuring what happens is good!

Spells of the Living

Samhain is a time to contemplate what you need to survive. Smart witches use any Samhain energy they can to make the winter more bearable!

The Needfire Spell

A needfire is a bonfire used to kindle magickal energy for a specific purpose, usually a serious survival need. Deep-seated needs belong in this fire: wishes for someone to recover his or her good health from an especially dangerous illness, requests for money to get through the winter (so as to keep the heat from getting shut off), and even for a new home if there is no current dwelling or if the current dwelling makes inadequate winter shelter.

If you live in a place where you can easily access a fire pit, get what you need to start a fire and bring jugs of water to extinguish it. Also, make sure you have paper, pens, a list of needs, and offerings of dried herbs (chamomile, marigold flowers, and rosemary are appropriate). Establish the fire area as a sacred space, and then start the fire. Once you have it burning steadily, write down different needs on a piece of paper and then throw it into the fire, saying "Spirit of the Samhain flame, see to these needs in the coming year!" Follow the needs with an offering. When finished, meditate on the fire until it starts dying down. Make sure you put the fire out totally before leaving.

A Spell to Settle Old Debts

One Irish proverb says "everyone has debts on Halloween." Since Samhain is a time of the old going out and the new coming in, this is an excellent time to call on magick for help in settling your own arrears. These days, everyone has them, whether the standard mortgage payment, that persistent student loan, or that credit card bill left over from a month when your car broke down.

For this spell, you'll need a heatproof container, some copies of bills you've already paid, and a sturdy banishing herb such as Solomon's seal, marjoram, or a few twigs trimmed from a lilac bush. Perform this spell outdoors or in a well-ventilated space if possible.

Put the bill in the container and light it, chanting:

> *As these bills burn,*
> *chains melt,*
> *debts be fed,*
> *debts be dead.*
> *The money I earn*
> *I keep for myself!*

As each bill burns, add a few pieces of your chosen herb. Repeat this spell every month until the debts are paid.

Spell against Sorrow

One of the reasons we practice divination at Samhain is that its messages come through with the most clarity. We also do it because we want some reassurance, any we can get really, that everything will be okay. If you are worried about what might happen and feel like the previous years have taken enough, create this ward against sorrow before you perform any Samhain divinations.

For this spell, gather a hot glue gun, a piece of cardboard or posterboard, a fern branch, a sheer scarf, a few sewing pins, and either a medallion of Archangel Michael or an image of a deity you consider a protector. Each symbol is a ward against pain.

The fern: Keeps off old ghosts, inner and outer.

The image of Michael: Protects from all harm; if you prefer not to call on angels, a deity from your own pantheon or a historic figure whom you respect and see as a protector will also work.

The scarf: Represents the veil of Isis, or the person brave enough to look beyond the veil between life and death itself. In this case, you are asking for things to stay behind that veil.

Glue the archangel symbol to the cardboard, then glue the fern branch so it frames the symbol. Wrap the scarf over top of these and pin it to the cardboard.

Take this image into your sacred space and speak sincerely, as you would to a trusted friend, about your recent troubles. Explain why you need a break right now. Hang it across from your front door, so that the image is behind you whenever you greet visitors.

Spell to Heal Grief

Samhain is the most sacred and often the most celebrated of the sabbats. In its sanctity comes a part that's difficult to celebrate: remembrance. When we remember, we feel. When we feel, we often grieve. Sometimes it's grief for someone dead; other times it's grief for what once was, for what never was, and for our own failures. These are all natural parts of the season, just as much as the joy and mystique.

Grief has its place in all of this, but sometimes mourning takes too much of our energy and instead of acting as a way to teach us what we value, it completely colors our worldview. These spells put grief in its proper place—informing us of what we've lost, so that we know what in life to cherish.

For this spell, gather together one glass of water, an amethyst, rose quartz, and hematite. Soak the stones in the glass overnight. Using each stone one at a time shake a little fluid over your head each morning, saying each time:

> *Lovely gem to wounded souls*
> *find and fill the aching holes.*
> *Set to right what grief has rent;*
> *further anguish, please prevent.*

Spell to Break an Ongoing Streak of Bad Luck

It seems like bad luck is never an isolated incident. You don't just get a parking ticket—you get a parking ticket, a tax notice, and you find out you need the roof repaired all on the same day. Bad luck is the streak that messes up life's paint job.

You can slow that streak with a very simple spell. All you need is table salt.

Pour three lines of salt on a table. All three must be equal in size. Circle your right arm around the salt, lean your head down, and say:

> *Blessed mother, who art eternal,*
> *cleanse my spirit of its maladies—*
> *let good come to me again.*

Sweep the salt away from you; do not reuse.

Spell to Assist in Creative Flow

For artists, winter is often their time of greatest production. However, the dark that comes with Samhain can sap the imagination and the cold can make curling up with a hot drink preferable to working. This spell helps keep the creativity flowing during those times when inertia might win. Take a little bit of that lingering summer energy with you into the dark side of the year so that you have some brightness from within to light your own creative path.

Gather a salt rock crystal, a bit of milk (animal or vegetable), and a cup or glass. Drop the rock crystal in the milk, saying:

> *Clear the mind,*
> *free the flow,*
> *mind aligned*
> *in creative glow.*

The milk will eat away the salt. As the salt melts, so does your creative block.

Spells of the Dead

While this season is a season of magick, it is also a season of honoring death, cherishing memory, and working with spirits. Pagans do not fear death more or less than anyone else. They do make an effort to accept and normalize it as part of nature. Magick that works with the dead, or that acknowledges inner death, helps with this process of acceptance. From communing with departed ancestors to sending psychological issues to their metaphorical graves, witches of all walks find ways to make use of the thinned veil.

A Spell to Speak with Your Ancestors

When the ancestors cross the veil, sometimes they do it in the form you remember. More often, however, they adopt forms as metaphors for what they want to communicate—a butterfly to tell you their soul survived, a breeze to suggest a direction for you to take, or sometimes a specific smell that you associate with that person. These forms may limit communication.

If you wish to apply trancework, however, you can engage a two-way conversation. If you try this, it's a good idea to have someone you trust nearby to check on you and keep you safe. Spend some time praying for the protection of your deity before you enter the trance to ensure that only ancestors with intents that align with yours appear.

Set up your sacred space with comfortable seating and a table with pictures and mementos of the ancestor or ancestors with whom you wish to communicate. Prepare a list of questions you might want to ask. You may also want to prepare some chamomile, mullein, and mugwort tea to help you relax.

After you set up the space, take a bath. Visualize any conflicting energy circling down the drain. Pause to anoint yourself with protection oil and say a few more prayers for protection as you do this work. Then don the clothing of your choice (comfortable is better) and prepare a small plate of food and a small beverage to offer your visiting ancestors. Bring this to the altar. Then, perform any rites that make a space sacred to you.

Sit down on your chair or pillows and take several deep breaths, as many as you need, until you feel yourself relaxing. At that point, announce to the ancestors that you would like to converse with them this evening. Say no more. Resume your deep breathing, paying calm attention to what you hear, see, smell, and feel.

When you feel you have completed your ritual, thank the ancestors for their time and ask them to return to the place they came from, expressing your love and gratitude for crossing the veil to come see you.

Give yourself a few moments to write down any information you felt important. When finished, open your sacred space, throw away or bury the food offerings, and take part in some lively, life affirming activity.

The Hell Money Spell

While we often think about our ancestors as omnipresent and possibly omniscient, some traditions assume that the ancestors have afterlives of their own to worry about, too. In China, people find ways to provide for their departed relatives. Hell money is paper money intended for the dead. You can buy some from an Asian grocery store or you can design and print your own. When you burn this money, it is believed that it goes to the afterlife, so that the departed can participate in the economy of the underworld. If you decide to send money to your ancestors, make sure you send it in big bundles—inflation is ridiculous in the land of the dead!

You can perform this spell as an act of reciprocation to grandparents or dead relatives who made sacrifices or enacted kindnesses for you while alive. Think of it as a way to thank grandparents for all the times they stuck a little extra money in your birthday card.

Hell money can also pay for support from elemental spirits, as a means of tipping them after they complete errands.

If you want to draw assistance to yourself, get a red drawstring bag, a magnet (one off your refrigerator will do), and a small note stating what you would like to attract. Carry this with you until what you want is part of your life. Once you have obtained your desire, the spell is complete. Keep the bag and magnet, and burn the hell money and the note. When a new need comes your way, simply add a new bill of hell money and a note and carry the bag again.

Protection Spells

According to folklore and modern news stories, Samhain/Halloween marks a dangerous season. The thinning veil tests our courage against the unknown, and the seasonal activities sometimes force us to stand back while our living beloveds take risks great and small as part of the merriment. Ease your worries a little by adding a few magickal protective measures alongside the day-to-day efforts.

Trick-or-Treating Protection

Every parent wants a safe child on Halloween night. While many do this by insisting on accompanying their children on trick-or-treating rounds, older children may want their independence. Along with reflective tape, flashlights, multiple exhortations about strange behaviors, and ignoring their protests and going with them anyway, add a few protective details to their costumes, shoes, and even in the bottom of their trick-or-treat buckets to prevent them from wandering into fairyland.

Sew this into their costume lining: Two sticks of rowan wood tied together with a red thread to form a plus sign. These days you can purchase sticks online. Faeries dislike rowan wood, so this will keep them off your children.

Glue this to the bottom of their treat bucket: Find a hag stone (a stone with a small natural hole through the center) and glue it on the inside bottom of the treat bucket. Troublesome spirits will steer clear of the candy. Then the only evil to combat will be whatever lies in too much sugar.

Threshold Magick

Threshold magick addresses vulnerability we expose ourselves to daily: that which lies between. When we think of thresholds, we think mainly of doors and windows. But thresholds cover far more than that; bridges, curbs, fences, and even water inlets serve as spaces between two worlds. Each of these is magickally powerful and a place where you are vulnerable. These spots align with the veil by literally cutting a space between one thing and another, usually the inside world of the home and the outside world of the wild universe. The following spells and practices help you seal off some of those vulnerabilities.

Samhain House Blessing

Ancient Pagans often prepared for Samhain with intense cleaning and organizing. This was to honor their visiting ancestors by presenting themselves at their best. It likely also made the winter work all the easier to do, as they had just reviewed where they put everything!

Nowadays, Samhain is still an excellent time for house cleansing and blessing. It gives you a chance to scoot out stagnant energy, and to weave in protective wards and blessings throughout your home.

This spell is really a series of spells, and depending on the square footage of your home, you may want to work on one floor per day over a series of several days, or one room per day, especially if you have a lot of clutter. You will need garbage bags to package and remove clutter, whether donating or discarding. You will also need a smudge stick or spray, a dark blue candle, a plate and small offerings of food, a candle of any color you like as an offering, and a spray bottle filled with saltwater.

House cleansing can take place at any time and is always beneficial. For best results, repeat cleansings and blessings once a month. It includes the following steps:

1. Physical cleaning
2. Smudging/cleansing by air
3. Smudging/cleansing by fire
4. Smudging/cleansing by water and earth
5. Making an offering to the household deities/to the deities to which you pray, asking for their blessing and protection on your household.

A Samhain cleansing should also include placing a ward on all the doors, windows, sources of information, and sources of transportation.

After clearing clutter as much as you can, smudge the room with white sage or a stick of frankincense incense. If you are allergic to incense smoke, you may smudge the room using a sprayer filled with a tea made from the sage or other cleansing herbs such as lemongrass and rosemary. Ask that the smoke or scent render each piece of energy it touches clean and healthy.

Follow this by lighting a dark blue candle and walking to every corner of your home, asking that the light seal your home from harm of any kind.

Set the candle in a heatproof dish on your stove and allow it to burn down. Then use the spray bottle to spritz every corner, door, and window in your home, calling on water and earth to combine its powers so that those with good intentions can enter easily and those with bad intentions find themselves distracted from entering.

Once you have finished preparing your home with this blessing, light the offering candle and lay out some food and drink on your stove (the modern equivalent of the hearth), addressing prayers to the deities of most importance in your home and asking for their protection as they remove all troublesome energies and spirits.

Garage Protection Spell

In historic rural Ireland and Scotland, scores of spells revolved around protecting barns and livestock. Pagan farm owners may well still use those spells. Since the advent of the automobile, magickal people may also in turn apply barn magick to their garage, as it protects one of our primary and most costly forms of transportation.

You will need to visit a source of running water. While a natural source is preferable, if you live somewhere landlocked you can use a public fountain or simply run your tap.

Take a silver coin (a silver dollar is ideal) and a quartz crystal. Dip the coin into running water, envisioning the molecules of the water and the coin comingling and becoming part of one another. Take the coin and the crystal and glue or tape it to the inside of your garage door or to the ceiling of your garage.

You may want to keep a second coin and crystal in a jar of your source water. When it comes time to renew house blessings and defenses, anoint the mounted crystal and coin with the water to refresh its energy.

A Spell for Protection from the Dark

The darkness of Samhain season is a tricky thing. It gives us an opportunity to work magick that doesn't play well with the light of day. On the other hand, that darkness is with us everywhere, as are strange creatures of the night lurking in our psychic shadows. Rather than jump at every shadow you face, give yourself a rest with a bit of coral and jet.

Take each stone and speak to it as though it's a person who can hear you. Say you need protection, the sorts of things you need protection from, and that they can do this job. If you have time, leave them in a moonlit window during the full three days of the full moon, talking to the stones about their assigned jobs during the daylight hours.

After you have sufficiently blessed and activated the stones, stitch them into your gloves or into some other piece of clothing you wear often. They will protect you from the weird things lurking in the dark so that you may go about your business.

Love Spells

The idea of Samhain being a time of love spells might seem strange to us nowadays. After all, who wants to flirt with a stranger with your dear departed grandma looking on? It seems, though, that Grandma might help you pick right. Back in the old days, fire festivals were premiere social occasions that played an important role in matchmaking. Hence, most of the divinations of the season concerned discovering the identity of a future spouse. We live longer and so our priorities surrounding love are different now; some of us seek life companionship, others a friend for a season. Samhain, because of its between-the-words nature, best suits spells for enduring love and friendship.

A Love Uncrossing Spell

If you feel like your love life carries some curse or karmic burden, try this to lift it. It may not replace the basic need for therapy or for learning new ways to think about emotional connection, but it is a great way to set the intention of trying to be different with love in the new year.

Gather a purple or black candle, a heatproof plate or bowl, blank paper, a marker, rue oil or a pinch of olive oil with rue stirred in, a nail or pencil, and one of your own hairs.

Set the plate in the center of your sacred space. Draw a figure eight on the piece of paper. Mark five plus marks inside the figure on both sides, for a total of ten marks. Carve your own name on the candle and run oil on it from the end to the wick. Place your hair on top of the seal and the candle over top. Light the candle. As it burns, chant seven times:

> Samhain day to Samhain night,
> take away my own heart's blight.
> Free my heart from seals and blocks;
> the world of love now unlocks!

Allow the candle to burn for seven minutes a day. When gone, carry the seal in a pocket or in your wallet.

A Spell to Release Old Loves of the Past

Sometimes what keeps you moving forward is affection lingering from your past. Samhain, at a time where time itself is in an in-between phase, is an excellent time to release that energy. By letting go of old karmic bonds, you gift yourself a chance to move forward with your life.

You will need a cord or a piece of twine that is large enough to tie around your waist with an additional two feet of cord remaining. Also, get some lemongrass essential oil for after your work. To make sure that these changes are irreversible, rub a little walnut oil on your fingers.

Since spells of release act as cleansing ceremonies, make sure you take a bath beforehand, concentrating on all you want to send to the beyond. Once you have bathed, dress comfortably and establish your sacred space. Take the cord around your waist, and while around you, add timber hitch knots to tie the ends together, adding one knot for each relationship energy you intend to release. As you tie each knot, think about a specific person and the intense memories, connections, and feelings you carry for that person. Take care to remember both the good and the bad thoroughly. Follow this process for each knot until you no longer have any remaining cord.

Spread your arms and legs apart, imitating Da Vinci's Vitruvian man, and close your eyes. Visualize the way these energies bind you and how they disrupt the flow of energy between you and the greater universe. Once you feel this energy as viscerally as you can, pick up the last knot you tied, and untie it. Take a few deep breaths as the energy from that bind flows back out into the universe and out of your life.

When you have untied all the knots, let the rope drop from your waist to the floor. Rub your hands and your solar plexus in a lemongrass-scented oil, taking deep breaths as the oil soaks into your skin. Then anoint the crown of your head, your heart, and your belly, giving yourself a fresh capacity to connect to others in a loving way. After cleaning your sacred space, you should either burn or bury the cord.

Faery Magick

Faery Magick involves a complicated dance between protection from faeries and cooperation with them. There are many theories about what they are but no one knows exactly. What we do know is that when the veil thins, Samhain becomes the time that belongs to them. We also know that faeries are more diverse than cute winged creatures; just because they appear as charming does not mean that they actually are. Some people, based on their cultural upbringing, want to avoid faeries. Others want to embrace them. What follows leaves room for both worldviews.

A Spell to Prevent Faery Theft or Nightmares

Many legends forewarn that the faeries may try to steal children. In addition, scary movies are often popular at this time of year, and the images a child or adult might take to bed can lead to some troubled sleep. This spell covers both problems.

It should stop a faery from trying to steal your child (or you!) and it prevents nightmares after that ten-hour *American Horror Story* marathon.

All you need is a hag stone. A hag stone is simply a stone with a naturally worn hole through the center. These used to be difficult to obtain unless you lived near a beach in the United Kingdom; these days, however, you can order them online. Hang it above the bed on a string or mount it on a piece of cardboard with glue. Above it, attach two long iron nails that cross each other in the middle. The nightmares will sweep through the hole and errant faeries won't come near you!

A Spell to Make the Faeries Welcome

If you want the faeries in your home, make it habitable to them. Pick a corner by a door or window, and set a cup and saucer there. Place a hollowed eggshell inside. (You can do this by using a sewing pin to poke holes on either end of the egg and then blow the yolk out.) Leave out a thimble filled with milk every day. When you take the thimble outside, take a few minutes to chat with your prospective tenant about house rules. Please note that this only works with animal milk. Faeries take compacts seriously; if you make a promise, follow through or face unpleasant consequences.

A Spell to Claim a Hive of Bees

There are those who believe that some tales of faeries are metaphors for vegetation spirits. This metaphor is especially likely in the case of bees. Nowadays, any magick at all to propagate them is a good thing. So if a swarm of bees appears on land that you happen to grow food on, put on gloves and sprinkle some foxglove seeds or leaves and lay claim to them, saying:

> These bees are mine,
> part of my land!

The Scottish Highlanders saw unclaimed bees as bad luck, so claim them, as to have them nowadays is lucky!

Divination

When the veil thins between worlds, it also thins the lines between past, present, and future. This makes it an excellent time to pull out tarot cards or play games of fate. For those who prefer quiet evenings indoors on Samhain night, try these methods to pass the time and plan the future.

The Thimble Spell

Right before bed, take a sewing thimble and scoop salt into it. Then walk backward from your bedroom door to your bed. When you lie down, grasp the thimble firmly between your thumb and forefinger. Gaze at it until you need sleep. This will fix the thimble in your mind as a dream symbol and anchor. The salt will make you thirsty. In your dreams, the person who gives you a beverage will also be your next lover.

The Kale Dream to See Your Future Spouse

Cabbage and kale played greatly into old Halloween traditions. Young people would sneak into a neighbor's yard at midnight and pull a kale stalk. The kale would then be hung over a doorway overnight (to charge it with some threshold magick, possibly) and then the next morning someone would examine the roots, leaves, and soil for traits of that person's future spouse. Unfortunately, records are inconsistent as to what plant detail translated to what in terms of spousal fortunes.

You don't need to steal your neighbor's kale to perform this divination, nor do you need some esoteric knowledge of leaf quality. If you happen to grow kale, or have a local source handy, try this spell.

First, make a kale stew. If you are not normally a kale fan and want to try this, make ramen noodles and stir in the kale. Allow it to become cold.

Go to your bedroom just before bed. Hold the pot of cold kale and stand on something you have never stood on before. (A towel will do.)

Say nine times:

Hot kale, cold kale, help me see
who I might marry
and who might marry me.

Drink nine times from the stew, set the pot aside, and then walk backward into your bed. You will dream of your future spouse. Dispose of the stew in the morning.

The Nut Crack Divination

This old Scottish tradition helped gents and ladies make up their minds when they had more suitors than they could handle. Take three nuts and set them over an open flame (or in a frying pan.) Name one nut for yourself, and name the other nuts for your sweethearts. If the nuts jump closer to your nut, they are more inclined toward you. If the nut cracks or jumps often, the lover is untrustworthy. The closer a nut burns to yours, the more likely marriage will follow. You can also use this as a means of divining which of your friends are most trustworthy.

The Divination of the Three Plates

This variation on blindman's buff is a Scottish divination. You will need a blindfold and three plates: one filled with grain (meal was traditional), one filled with soil, and one with any type of net. Blindfold the person and turn him or her around three times, then let that person's hand fall on a plate. This will foretell what comes in the next year.

The meal/grain stands for prosperity, the soil for death (which often indicates dramatic not usually literal changes), and the net for tangled fortunes (what we of the modern day call "drama").

A Rune Spell to Change Your Fate

A few things in life are fated. Most, however, you can change. This spell is all about rewriting your fate, at least when there isn't some life lesson written in what's already coming.

You will need a set of runes, a plate to rest them on, mugwort, and a dictionary that details rune meanings if you do not already have them memorized. You may also wish to make an offering or write a letter of petition to the Fates or the face of fate in your specific tradition.

In your sacred space, take out three runes that represent the situation at hand or the three runes that troubled you when you gave yourself a reading. Set those out on the plate.

Next, set the runes that represent your desired outcome on top of the original runes. Surround these with mugwort. Visualize the runes glowing, eventually making the energy of the runes beneath them dust—where only your desired fate remains. Leave the runes undisturbed in their herbal circle for three days.

Samhain is a time when all things are possible. It is also a time to create new possibilities. Use this time as the ground grows colder to shape what might greet you in the spring. The air is rich with magick, so use this time to partake of that particular fruit!

RECIPES
AND
CRAFTS

...th, bereavement, ... ancestry, courage, beginnings, endings, ...

...arnation, wisdom, survival, preservation, hunting, other worlds, ...

...ing, release from old bonds, road openings, fire, protection, sun ...

... of scorpio, sun sign of scorpio, dark moon, pleiades at highe...

...at midnight, the crone, the grieving mother, the grieving wife, ...

...ter, Persephone and Hades, Ereshkigal, Osiris, Janus, Cer...

...nunnos, the Daghda, Hecate, Dis Pater, Hel, Inanna, ...

..., Lilith, Macha, Maui, the Morrigan, Osiris, Isis, ...

Rhiannon, Samana, Teutates, Taranis, the Horned God, the ...

...orange, brown, yellow, grey, green, cedar, dittany of crete, sag...

...orn, wheat, rye, pumpkins, hazel, hemlock, chrysanthemum, ...

...rigold, jet, obsidian, onyx, carnelian, moonstone, iron, black ...

...s, owls, ravens, decaying leaves, myrrh, copal, death, wheel of ...

... priestess, cauldron, mask, besom, apple, pumpkin, fermented ...

...raut, pickled eggs, pickled beets, roasted nuts, raw nuts, apple...

...wood, divination, soul cakes, sugar skulls, jack-o-lanterns, b...

...bbing, seances, scrying, bonfires, trick-or-treating, mummer's...

...e off gravesites, dedicate memorials, visit nursing homes, sam...

...alan gaef, calan gaef, gealach a ruadhain, calan gaef, kala...

$\mathcal{S}$AMHAIN HAS SUCH rich visual and sensual themes that some people don't want to put the skeletons back in their closet when it's over! If you prefer gothic motifs for your home, this is certainly the season to shop. If you're someone who prefers to change decor to reflect the seasons, take advantage of Halloween's commercial popularity, whether you go ready-made or handmade. You can grab the last of the late harvest foods for your ancestral meal and stock up on black candles and no one will think twice about any cackling as you do it! While Halloween may have a reputation for all the sugar highs, there are plenty of traditional dishes that allow you to sidestep the excess sweetness and embrace the season.

Recipes

The last of the harvest comes in just before Samhain. The dishes of Samhain are often an effort to use up the food that did not get preserved and to make the most of fresh food while you can. Kale, apples, nuts, and grains form the flavor of rich Halloween traditions.

Kale Chips

Kale, in recent years, has become a health food darling. It is also integral to Samhain—it still grows late into the fall—should you sneak into someone's yard and steal a kale stalk to see what kind of person you might marry, you might as well eat it when done!

Just because kale is healthy does not mean you can't enjoy it. This recipe poses it as a replacement for the potato chip. It may take a few tries as you figure out at what temperature your oven plays best with the plant, but once you master that, you can revel in the happy crunch of a well-toasted leaf.

Ingredients:
1 bunch of kale
2 tablespoons olive or sunflower oil
Sea salt, to season to taste

Preheat your oven to 275°F. Thoroughly wash the kale, then remove the center stem (also called the rib), and cut leaves into 1 inch or larger pieces. You may wish to blot any excess water. Toss in a bowl with the oil until the kale has an even coating. Sprinkle with sea salt. Bake for 10 minutes or until crisp, then flip over and bake the other side.

Serve hot or cold. Another option is to flavor the chips with a favorite spice mix before baking.

Baked Apples

Apples are everywhere at Samhain, used in games such as bobbing and biting, for apple peel divinations, and for pulling apart in tests of strength.

Ingredients:

Apples, cored—one for each person you are serving
1 tablespoon maple syrup (per apple)
1 tablespoon raisins (per apple)
1 teaspoon allspice, cinnamon, or ground cloves (per apple)

Set the cored apples in a ramekin or glass dish on a microwave safe plate. In a bowl, mix the raisins, maple syrup, and spices until evenly distributed. Fill the apple. Microwave on high for 2 minutes per apple.

If using an oven: Preheat oven to 375°F. Bake filled apples in a glass dish or in individual cups for 10 to 13 minutes.

Apple Curry Soup

This may look vaguely like applesauce, but it's much more complex.

Ingredients:
5–6 large apples, cored and sliced into ¼ inch pieces
2 cups water
2 tablespoons sweet curry
1 tablespoon lemon juice
1 teaspoon allspice
1 teaspoon chili powder

Combine all the ingredients in a crockpot and cook on low overnight. In small batches, pour ingredients into a food processor and puree. Pour the puree back into the pot and reheat for an hour. Serve warm.

Pumpkin Seeds

Pumpkins are ubiquitous at Samhain season, so much so that it's easy to be overwhelmed. While pumpkin pie is usually the first and favorite go-to, you can try pumpkin in just about any recipe that calls for squash, or use it in your favorite baking recipe as a substitute for butter and sometimes as a substitute for flour. (This will take some trial and error.)

The rule for pumpkin seeds is this: the bigger the pumpkin, the bigger the seeds. That also comes with the price of pulp. There is, however, a way to remove that pulp without losing your mind.

When you clean out the pumpkin pulp, place the seeds and pulp in a large bowl. Rinse under running water, picking out the large pieces of pulp as you go. Repeat this process a few times, removing the pulp as able. Once you have gotten as much as you can from this method, fill the bowl with as much water as it can contain. The seeds will float to the top, while the pulp sinks. You can then skim out and dry the seeds off with a bit of paper towel.

Ingredients

1–2 cups of pumpkin seeds

1–2 teaspoons of olive or sunflower oil

Salt to taste

Preheat oven to 300°F. In a bowl, toss the seeds with oil and then salt to taste. Spread seeds evenly on a baking sheet. Bake for about 45 minutes, checking and stirring every 15 minutes to ensure even browning.

Allow to cool. Eat as a snack or use as a garnish in salads, soups, and sandwiches.

Pumpkin Puree

While many cooks prefer to get their pumpkin puree from a can, it often comes preseasoned in ways that do not cooperate with dishes besides desserts. To make this, you will need to cook the pumpkin shell. You will need at least one small pumpkin to make the puree.

Ingredients
1–2 small pumpkins

Preheat oven to 350°F. Slice the top off a small pumpkin. Then scoop out the innards like you would any squash. Rinse off the flesh pieces, cutting them into 5- or 6-inch slices, and spread them out on a baking sheet. Bake for 45 minutes; check about halfway through to make sure they brown instead of burn. Remove and cool until you can touch them comfortably. At this point, you can easily peel off the pumpkin skin with your hands, using a knife to scrape off any small, stubborn bits.

Place the remaining shell in a blender or a food processor a few pieces at a time and puree. Add a little water as you do this to ensure a smooth blend. You may wish to work over the puree with a potato ricer after it goes through the food processor to smooth out any remaining chunks. You can freeze this until you need it.

Pumpkin Bisque

Ingredients:

1 whole onion, chopped

1 clove garlic, minced

1 ½ tablespoons butter

1 cup pumpkin puree

1 ¼ cup water

½ teaspoon cinnamon

½ teaspoon chili powder

A few strands of saffron (optional)

1 cup whole milk unsweetened yogurt

In a saucepan, sauté the onions and garlic in butter until they brown. Add the pumpkin puree, water, and spices and boil. Reduce heat immediately and simmer for five minutes, gradually adding the yogurt. Serve warm.

Pan de Muerto (**Bread of the Dead**)

Bread is the ultimate ancestral food: it is the marker of human agricultural history. It represents the point at which humans began to inhabit one area of land for a long time, and the time at which they changed their diets from hunter-gatherer to farmed fare. In Samhain, breads and cakes bore many traditions ranging from fortune telling to faery pacts. Now, it's another tasty treat, whether we keep it to ourselves or share.

This bread is often served as part of *Dia de Los Muertos* celebrations as an offering of food to the departed ancestors that their families may also enjoy. What makes it tricky is that the baker rolls it into something resembling a skeleton shape before baking. You may want to practice on clay or playdough a few times before you make this!

Ingredients:

½ cup milk

6 tablespoons unsalted butter, cut to ½ inch pieces

¼ teaspoon orange juice

1 tablespoon orange blossom water

3 large eggs, lightly beaten

¼ teaspoons active dry yeast

3½ cups unbleached all-purpose flour

½ cup granulated sugar (coconut sugar also works here)

1 teaspoon salt
Sunflower oil as needed
Butter, honey, powdered sugar (optional)

Preheat oven to 350°F. In a saucepan, melt together the milk, butter, and orange juice.

Take off of heat and cool until it feels safe to touch. Add the orange blossom water and whisk in the eggs. Add yeast to this mixture. Let the mixture stand until it bubbles slightly, usually in three or four minutes.

On a clean, flat work surface, mix together the flour, sugar, and salt. Make a small mound out of the mix, and then with your finger create a well in the center of it. Add a little bit of the milk and yeast mixture, working the flour, and pausing to add a little bit more in at a time until the liquid and solids are incorporated. Knead until the dough is only a little bit sticky. Add flour as necessary.

Put the dough in a large oiled bowl and cover with a clean dishtowel. Leave in a warm spot until the dough doubles in size. This usually takes about an hour.

Making the Skeleton Parts:

Set aside a portion of the dough—the size of two dinner rolls is good. Divide the remaining dough onto two greased or lined baking sheets and flatten. Use the reserved dough to shape your skeletal impressions. There is no specific rule for how to shape the skeleton—you might shape all the dough into a single skull and then use your fingers to shape a face.

You could also separate the dough into two larger balls and one smaller ball. On one of the two larger balls, roll out a pillar, and then shape the ends like a cartoon bone. Repeat this on the other large piece of dough, and then lay that bone over the top of the other bone in the form of a cross. Take the smaller piece of dough and roll it into a ball. Use your thumbs to push two eye impressions into one area, and with a toothpick shape out the nose holes and teeth. If you check sites such as allrecipes. com for *pan de muertos*, you will see that cooks generally go for the impression of a skeleton rather than a precise creation.

Once you have shaped the dough as you wish, place the bread on the center rack of the oven, cooking for 30–40 minutes or until golden brown.

You may wish to garnish the bread after with a brush of melted butter and honey or powdered sugar.

Sugar Skulls

Unlike *pan de muertos*, sugar skulls are intended only as food for the dead. After making them, place them on the gravesites of departed loved ones or leave them outside for the elements to consume. (If you live in an area with fire ants or bees, choose a place far from any residence to leave them.) Also, since sugar is much more difficult to shape than bread, invest in a silicon mold for this. Try to get the more realistic/toothy type mold—the cartoonish skull and crossbones shapes tend to crumble on the way out! Also, choose a low humidity day to make these, otherwise the ingredients may crumble and lose their shape.

This recipe is intended for a small batch mold, rather than for larger skull molds that are also available.

Ingredients:
1 cup sugar
1 teaspoon meringue powder or cream of tartar
1 teaspoon of water (or more, may need to add as you go)
Colored icings, beads, feathers, etc. for decorating

In a large bowl, mix the sugar and the meringue powder. Sprinkle in a teaspoon of water until you can press your thumb into the mixture and the print remains. Fill the mold with this mixture, pressing the back and ensuring it's as flat as possible. Make sure to leave a sliver of space at the back of the mold—this makes it easier to remove the skull intact. You may want to use a butter knife to ensure that the back of each mold remains flat. Flip the mold over onto a flat plate. If using a silicon mold, you can lightly press the face of the mold for a release. With a plastic mold, you may need to tap with the flat side of the butter knife. Allow the skulls to dry for 24 hours. After they have dried completely, use the icing and other tools to decorate as you wish. If attaching nonedible elements, use the icing as glue. Allow to dry another 24 hours, and then they are ready as offerings!

A sugar skull

Soul Cakes

In the British Isles, the poor often went to prosperous houses on Samhain night seeking aid in the form of food, money, and prayers, and they offered prayers in return. Often the people visited provided soul cakes, as a sort of payment for the prayers and blessings that they offered to their dead. This dry cookie makes a nice addition to any dumb supper you wish to host.

Ingredients:

3 eggs

2 cups flour (almond and oatmeal flour make good substitutes)

½ teaspoon cinnamon

½ teaspoon nutmeg

½ teaspoon salt

½ cup milk

½ cup sugar or maple syrup

1 stick butter

½ cup raisins

Preheat oven to 400°F. Beat one egg and set aside. In a small bowl, combine the flour and spices. In a saucepan, heat milk until hot to the touch. In a mixer, cream together the sugar and butter. Add the egg yolks of the remaining two eggs and blend ingredients thoroughly. Add in the flour and mix on high until the mixture crumbles. Gradually add the milk until a soft dough forms.

Turn the dough out on a flat, clean surface and knead until it is uniform. Roll into a cylinder, then cut into roughly half-inch slices. Lay out on a baking sheet and brush with the reserved beaten egg.

Bake for 15 minutes, until golden brown.

Griddle Cakes

The Irish often served griddle cakes on Samhain and All Souls' Day. These, much like pancakes, go best with syrup and hot butter.

Ingredients:
2 cups flour
¾ teaspoon baking soda
½ teaspoon salt
1 cup whole milk or yogurt
Sunflower oil

Sift the dry ingredients together, taking time to whisk with a fork so that the powder blends fine. Add the milk or yogurt a little bit at a time until a dough forms. Shape the dough into 2-inch circles about ½-inch thick. Fry in 1 tablespoon of sunflower oil in frying pan over medium heat; make sure to brown on both sides.

Colcannon (Irish Stew)

Colcannon is an Irish stew once popularly served on Samhain in Ireland. It was also featured in several different divination and magick traditions of the time, perhaps because it typically included potatoes and kale. A potato masher makes this recipe much easier, but a fork and determination can get the job done.

Ingredients:
1 head of kale or cabbage, with leaves sliced thin
1 stick butter, divided into three parts
1 cup of milk
7–8 potatoes, peeled and chopped
1 tablespoon chives for garnish

Cover the kale with water and boil until it wilts but the leaves remain green, about thirty minutes. Drain the water and chop the kale into fine slivers. In the same pan, over medium heat, add one third of the butter. As it melts, stir in the kale. Add the milk and bring to a light boil. Next, add the potatoes, mashing them with a fork while they cook. As the potatoes soften, the mashing becomes easier. The potatoes are done when they have the same consistency as mashed potatoes. Add the next third of butter. Make a center in the resulting potato mound and add the last third of the butter.

Add any garnishes and serve warm.

Lamb's Wool

Think of this beverage as the Scottish answer to sangria. While the flavoring varied by geography and preference in Great Britain, Lamb's Wool typically consisted of half ale and half cider, heated with what spices were available. If you have a crockpot or even a pot on your stove, you can give this a try.

Ingredients:
Ale, light
Cider
1 teaspoon cloves
1 teaspoon cinnamon

Stir together the ale and cider. Add the herbs. Bring to a simmer. Serve warm.

Crafts

Halloween and Samhain abound with crafting opportunities. Along with creating your own pieces of art to fill your home with a loving, spooky spirit, you can also turn crafts into magickal tools. After all, function following form is how many a kitchen and hedge witch operates! You can go kid-friendly with simple crafts that require basics such as glue, Popsicle sticks, and paint, or you can go advanced while using scoring knives and grownup glue such as Mod Podge. Think about your home and the way you practice faith and magick. Think about the type of Samhain celebration you want to have and then create accordingly!

Pumpkin Crafts

No vine appears so prolific as the pumpkin in autumn. From mini versions to fruits larger than a mastiff, any person can find something that suits the scale of his or her decorating ambitions. Thanks to their extreme abundance, many crafters and artists have come up with all sorts of innovative ways to use pumpkins in creative expression.

The carved pumpkin originates with the Irish tradition of carving turnips and beets. When the Irish came to the New World, pumpkins became their preferred Hallows night lamps.

Nowadays, jack-o'-lanterns still sit on many a porch, though in some areas they often fall victim to Halloween vandals. If you live in an area where your pumpkins might go untouched, you can go ahead and scoop and carve per tradition, or you can try some new methods of pumpkin crafting.

Scoring: Pin or tape a desired pattern to your pumpkin. Use the linoleum cutter to cut the surface skin of pumpkin along the lines of the pattern. Remove the paper and scrape off the remaining skin with a spoon, taking care not to cut through the pumpkin.

Decoupage: If you decide to decoupage your pumpkin, you will be painting it with glue. If you do this, you will have to give up eating it later—while the glue might be nontoxic, it's hard to tell what is in the items you glue to the pumpkin.

Before you begin, you may want to dilute your glue with water. This makes the liquid thinner and easier to work with, especially when painting it on a large surface. Proportions for dilution are a matter of personal taste. In any empty container (don't use one you use for food) pour out a little glue and add a little bit of water. Try adding 1/8 teaspoon water for every tablespoon of glue; add more water as you see fit.

You will need:
Newspapers or a drop cloth
A container for water
Glue, such as Mod Podge

Brushes or rollers

Items you wish to glue on your pumpkin (i.e., small charms, paper printouts, magazine cut outs, and/or strips of fabric)

An acrylic spray

Hot glue gun (optional)

Scissors

In a well-ventilated workspace, lay down the newspaper or drop cloth. Set out a container of water to dilute the glue. Pick one section of the pumpkin and add a light layer of glue with a brush or roller. Once you have coated the pumpkin, add the paper or fabric you want in that section. Add an additional layer of glue over top. You may need to pause to roll out wrinkles in the paper or gently straighten bumps that appear as the glue dries using light pressure with your finger. Once you have applied the paper and glue to the first section of the pumpkin, rotate and repeat until you have finished. You may wish to add a few additional layers of glue to all sides of the pumpkin. The glue will dry clear, so paint it over the top of the images. Allow the glue to dry overnight. Take the pumpkin to a well-ventilated place, such as a porch or garage and coat it with the acrylic spray. Allow to dry, and then add an additional layer of acrylic. Allow this to dry overnight. If you wish, after, use a hot glue gun to apply charms, beads, or small toys to the pumpkin. Allow to dry overnight, and then place it where you wish to display it.

Decoupaged pumpkin

Print: If you would like a fast and dirty way to decorate a pumpkin, just print on it. All you need is a permanent marker and a few words in mind. Write on your pumpkin in large letters. You might want to be quirky, leaving messages like "Eat at Joe's," or go referential, such as "Nevermore." If you have the skill, you may want to draw silhouettes or even sketch portraits. Write a poem, tell a story, or just leave instructions for package delivery.

Pin It: Pumpkins have spongy tissue with the same consistency as cork. You can use it as a de facto corkboard or even spell a few things out with pins. Pick a side of the pumpkin and push in pins or tacks. Get creative and make shapes, faces, runes, or even an image of a favorite tarot card!

Costumes

Part of the joy of Samhain comes from the chance to be someone else for a night; in a way, it is a form of travel, an opportunity to experience your everyday paths through the eyes of a different personality. Some Pagans incorporate costumes into a magickal practice called aspecting, where they temporarily assume a part of another consciousness. This happens most often in a Wiccan ceremony called Drawing Down the Moon. In this ritual, often the person steps aside and the goddess invoked takes charge. There are those who also practice a variation where they temporarily share consciousness with the deity—some see it as a magickal version of method acting.

Wearing costumes at Samhain dates back to the early Druids when villagers dressed up as animals. Commercial costumes, however, did not appear until the 1930s when the Irish in America began influencing the way all Americans celebrated Halloween.

If you want to explore a different perspective, explore a few different approaches to your costume, assembling it with your own sewing skills, or putting together items you find at garage sales and thrift shops.

A few ideas for a Samhain/Halloween costume:

1. Dress as a god or goddess that you work with on a regular basis.
2. Dress as an element of nature you are trying to learn and understand.
3. Dress as a historic or mythological witch or magician. Circe, Medea, Nicholas Flamel, Joan of Arc, Heinrich Agrippa are all connected to Samhain because of their contributions to magick and mysticism.
4. Dress as the personification of an abstract concept such as fear, love, mathematics, or quantum physics.

As you go about Samhain in costume, observe how taking on the new persona changes how you think and how you see the world. After the merriment, meditate on the lessons you took from the experience.

Make a Mask

If you don't want to go full-aspect but still want to try a change of perspective, make a mask. While again you can purchase a ready-made one, you can also make your own and adjust it to any worldview you want to experience.

You will need:
A blank mask template
Hot glue
Feathers, beads, ribbons

Glue the small items you have gathered around your mask in any pattern or configuration you like, taking care to leave room around the nose and eyes.

You can also make a mask with a paper bag.

You will need:
A grocery-size paper bag
Scissors
Crayons, paint, or markers
A stapler

A sewing tape measure

Sewing elastic, such as what might be used for the waist of a skirt or pants

Cut out an oval, square, or circle from the grocery bag. Make sure the oval is large enough to cover your face. Cut two eye-holes and a small slit around where you nose would go (to facilitate breathing). Decorate the mask with the crayons, paint, and so on. When finished, measure the circumference of your head and divide that by two. Use that measurement to decide how much elastic to cut. Staple each end of the elastic so that the ends of the staple will not touch your skin.

Spin Your Fears

This craft combines two magick-minded activities: meditation and divination. This simple wheel, made from a paper plate, gives you a playful way to explore the serious psychological aspects of the Samhain season.

You will need:

Construction paper

Scissors

A paper plate

Crayons or markers

A fastener, such as the type you get at an office supply store

Cut a small isosceles triangle out of the construction paper, which will become a pointer. Set that aside. Take a marker and divide the paper plate into at least four pie-shaped sections. In each section, write the name of a fear or a specific Samhain-related theme. Take the paper fastener and use it to attach the triangle to the plate. When ready to meditate on a topic, spin the triangle and focus on the theme it picks for you.

Make a Gravestone Rubbing

This craft requires a field trip. Go to an older cemetery, one where there are more upright stones. This method does not work quite as well on the newer grave markers as the modern markers have less texture.

You will need:
A large sheet of paper, such as what you can get from a
    jumbo drawing pad
A large crayon

Go to a cemetery and find a stone with an interesting pattern. Place the paper over the stone and rub the crayon sideways in short, fast motions until the stone pattern appears on the page. Fill up the page with the pattern. When finished, name the person on the memorial and say "thank you." Clean up the grave if it looks untended, and make sure to pick up after yourself.

Use these as part of your Halloween decorations, or, if you chose an ancestor's grave, make it part of an ancestral altar.

Gravestone rubbing

Make a Parshell

A parshell is a type of cross intended to protect children from mean-spirited faeries. While it came to be associated with the Christian cross, it predates its presence in Europe. It really works as more of an X type cross—a figure that can often stop outside magick in its tracks or seal magick of your own.

Parshell

You will need:
Two sticks—any type of wood is fine
Wheat stalks, rye stalks, or corn husk leaves
Twine

Cross the sticks to form a plus. Wrap the wheat stalks around the two sticks so that they weave together. Tie the twine along the same path as the wheat stems, adding a bowman's knot in the back to reinforce. Hang above your child's bed or even your own.

Samhain Ritual Crafts

Many Pagans have certain ritual items that they make themselves, either to save money or because what they need isn't easily available in stores. The following are just a few small things you might wish to make your own home ritual.

Samhain Oil

You will need:
1 tablespoon sunflower or olive oil
1 tablespoon calendula flowers
1 tablespoon marigold flowers
1 piece frankincense resin

Combine all the ingredients in a small bottle and leave in a sunny window until ready for use.

Samhain Loose Incense
Burn this herb mix over charcoal briquettes.

You will need:
1 teaspoon myrrh
1 teaspoon frankincense resin
1 teaspoon copal resin

Mix well. Burn a pinch at a time.

Samhain Bath Salts
You will need:
½ cup Epsom salt
½ cup sea salt
1 teaspoon vegetable glycerin
10 drops basil essential oil
10 drops camphor essential oil
11 drops vetiver essential oil

Pour the salts and glycerin into a shatterproof container (for safety in the bathroom.) Add the essential oils. Stir with a chopstick. Shake just before adding to water.

Samhain Divination Potion

Drink this potion right before you sit down to the tarot cards or play a traditional Samhain game. It helps relax you enough to accept and consider images from your subconscious mind without incapacitating you. Don't take this if you plan to drive within the hour.

You will need for one serving:
10 drops kava tincture
1 teaspoon mugwort
1 teaspoon meadowsweet
Dried orange peel to taste
1 cup boiling water

Assemble ingredients in a tea strainer. Steep for 7–13 minutes. Remove the strainer and ingredients; allow the tea to cool to a touchable temperature. Drink. Do not exceed three servings in an evening.

If you are looking for more Halloween and Samhain crafts, be sure to check your local library as well as websites such as Pinterest, CraftGawker, and About.com. Samhain is an inspiring season; you are bound to find some activity that suits your home and skill.

Decoration

Samhain is probably the most fun holiday for decorations. You can adopt a silly, spooky, or solemn motif—the approach should reflect how you plan to observe the holiday. Colors are the Halloween-emblematic orange and black or purple, though autumn spectrum colors such as red, brown, or yellow go well, too.

Go Spooky: If you wish to go spooky, you have endless choices. Retailers get almost as excited and excessive about Halloween as they do about Christmas! Throw artfully torn cheesecloth over all your furniture, hang fake spider webs from the corner (or just leave the ones that evolve naturally in place), and festoon flat surfaces with black candles, skulls, and pumpkins.

Go Solemn: You may prefer a more serious, muted observance. An ancestor's altar is one of the most profound forms of decor you can establish for Samhain. On a mantle or a table, display pictures of loved ones and personal heroes who have passed on. Add personal effects of those loved ones to that altar; these can be pieces of favorite candies, bottles of perfume, books, or even toys that you inherited. Throughout the month, you can write notes to your departed loved ones and place them on a bowl on the mantle. The rest of your house could continue with the decorations you set up for Mabon in muted fall tones, making Samhain in your house a meditation as much as a celebration.

Prepare a Path for the Ancestors

Slavic and Latin peoples both prepared for literal visits from their departed ancestors during Samhain season. People cleaned their homes, prepared lavish meals, and dressed in their nicest clothing. To formally host your own beloved dead, incorporate these traditions into your decor.

Those who celebrate *Dia de los Muertos* make an effort to help their ancestors find their way home. One way they do this is by lining their walkways with luminaries. Traditionally these are paper lanterns that cover candles. If you live in a windy area, however, candles may not stay lit. Fortunately, these days, small LED lights are available—you can even purchase the tea light style in packs. You can create simple luminaries by decorating brown paper bags with crayons or by cutting patterns into them and placing the lights inside. If you'd like to do a slightly different luminary path, try buying a series of small magnifying glasses and placing the lights just behind them. Since most LED candles flicker by design, this will create a play of light and shadow leading down the path to your door.

Ancestor Altars

Make your ancestors even more welcome by setting up an altar to honor them. Along with pictures of them from when they were alive, add small mementos from their lives. If they were not the type to collect items, you may want to write poems or put a Mason jar and paper out where you can write down small memories of the person to store in the jar.

If you live in a small space, a full altar might be difficult to maintain. In that case, try creating a mini-altar with a shadow box you can get from a craft store or make a terrarium style altar with miniature objects relating to the people in your family who you wish to honor. You need not buy special equipment for the terrarium, and it does not have to have plants. An inverted Mason jar or baby food jar will still work.

In addition to the altar, you might want to print out or create wall cutouts relating to family seals and family mottos from any known ancestral lines. For example, people of Scottish descent often had specific tartan patterns, and many families throughout Great Britain and Europe had family mottos and crests that represented their family heritage.

Dumb Supper Settings

If you plan to host a dumb supper, it is traditional to have a white tablecloth. Part of this tradition is that as your family toasts to the memories of the departed you spill a little on the cloth as an offering to them. Make sure it's a cloth you don't mind staining. Keep at least one seat empty; two or more is optimal. While eating in silence, pay attention to natural phenomena. Slavic peoples believed that anything from a breeze to the appearance of a moth during the dinner represented the presence of ancestor.

After the meal, set sugar skulls outside next to your luminaries (unless this will draw unwanted critters.) While adults give the skulls to children on the Day of the Dead, most do not eat them. Instead, they leave them outside on graves and tombs, so that the rain and other elements wear them away, allowing their ancestors to enjoy them.

Fend Off the Creatures of the Night

Perhaps you align with the old Irish tradition of keeping the frightening spirits of the night at bay. You can decorate your home to act as a fortress against the intruders. Decorate your front door with eyes—this looks like a play on Halloween spookiness but also represents turning back the evil eye and evil intentions. Line the walkway with cardboard headstones cut from shipping boxes. Instead of making them for celebrities or specific ancestors, put the names of the things that scare you on it; by symbolically putting these headstones in the ground, you take power over those fears. Use chalk to write protective incantations over your sidewalk, windows, and doors.

You could also write a faery story or a ghost story on your sidewalk or driveway, or perhaps quote poetry or phrases from Irish poet W. B. Yeats. If someone walking by stops to talk to you, invite that person to contribute to the story.

Decorate your windows with silhouettes and draw the shades as a backdrop. You can find printouts online of everything from bats and owls to the shadows of Victorian people. Add a wreath to your front door; in place of the usual fall leaves, make one from tissue paper flowers. Alternatively, you can make an iron wreath, gluing together old nails and screws into a circular pattern, or adding them to a premade straw wreath.

If you have sincere safety concerns, motion sensor toys that are popular and available during Halloween season come in handy. Place them at points around your home that you consider vulnerable. It will be an effective alert system if some living creature of the night attempts to make mischief.

Add a Little Hollywood Haunting

If your tastes run to the more modern, add references to your favorite scary or magickal movies and television shows. Print out stills from movies such as *The Serpent and the Rainbow* or *The Skeleton Key* and add a few elements from the movie to your decor and food, for instance, stringing actual skeleton keys in a garland. If you loved *Practical Magick*, serve margaritas.

Should you feel especially ambitious, decorate your space with a haunted movie theater theme. Hang thick curtains over your television and draw them closed when no one is watching. Hide rubber skeletons in coat and broom closets. Play up the silly spookiness by adding a fake trapdoor or set out a big, spooky book with random geometric patterns as an *Evil Dead* reference or create a shrine to Disney witches from Angela Lansbury to Angelina Jolie.

Divine the Future

If you prefer a less solemn celebration but still have some old-fashioned urbane tastes, set up your home to look like a Victorian divination parlor. Hang prints of vintage Halloween cards on the walls, especially those that refer to old superstitions. Gather fabric and ribbons to line stairwells and ledges with bunting. Place black netting over mirrors to make them look like they wear mourning veils. Use chalk to write names on your fireplace or at your stove, and hide tarot cards around your front room, challenging your guests to find all of them and put them together in readings of their own. Set up a table and chair in one corner of a room covered with a tablecloth in the style of the spiritualist mediums. Add printouts of spirit photography at different spots around the room. Incorporate references to Victorian era writers: Edgar Allan Poe, Mary Shelley, and Nathaniel Hawthorne were especially spooky.

Hang Mobiles

Mobiles are simple to make. All you need is a hanger, some string, a hole punch, and the material you wish to hang. Make a rune mobile, then whatever one a guest reaches up and grabs depicts that person's fortune. You might want to hang mobiles of apple shapes, as a reference to the game in which people tried to catch apples with their teeth. If you have a tarot deck with a few cards missing, this is a great way to give some life to the remaining deck.

Paper Doll Cutouts

Gather some old newspaper or use construction paper and cut out Halloween shapes. You can hang these garlands around your windows and along your ceilings. If your guests wish, let them take single pieces of the chain home to use in their own magick when seeking sweethearts, protection, or job promotions. You can find instructions online for producing different shapes in paper chains.

Make Your Own Halloween Wall Stickers

Find a pattern to trace, get some spray adhesive, shelf liner, and a box cutter. You can then make your own wall cutouts. Cut different shapes—perhaps the shapes of Victorian furniture to stick to your walls—to give the impression of two points in time happening at once in your living room for an extra feeling of seasonal spookiness.

You and your family may want to work out a way to celebrate both Halloween and Samhain. For Samhain, establish set traditions that honor your beloved dead. Those should stay more or less the same from year to year (though when big changes come, it will feel natural to change the way you practice, and that's okay.) For Halloween, change your approach from year to year and play with themes. It is possible to have fun and show some humor with the Samhain season, while still honoring its spiritual nature.

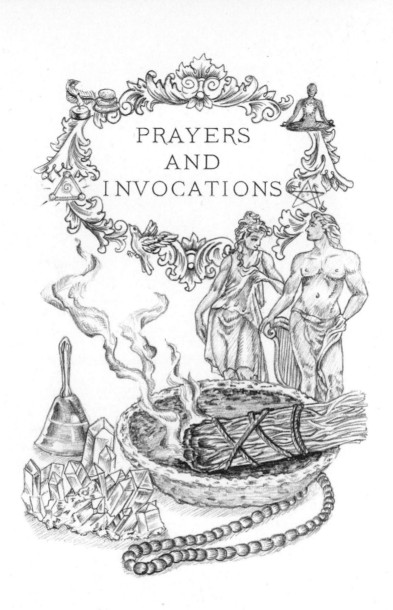

PRAYERS
AND
INVOCATIONS

... wisdom, survival, preservation, hunting, other worlds, faeri...

release from old bonds, road openings, fire, protection sun 15

...corpio, sun sign of scorpio, dark moon, pleiades at highest po...

...idnight, the crone, the grieving mother, the grieving wife, the wi...

...Persephone and Hades, Ereshkigal, Osiris, Janus, Cerridwe...

...os, the Daghda, Hecate, Dis Pater, Hel, Inanna, Ishtar...

...dith, Macha, Mare, the Morrigan, Osiris, Isis, Pomona...

...nnon, Samana, Teutates, Taranis, the Horned God, the wi...

...e, brown, yellow, grey, green, cedar, dittany of crete, sage, stra...

...wheat, rye, pumpkins, hazel, hemlock, chrysanthemum, calendu...

...ld, jet, obsidian, onyx, carnelian, moonstone, iron, black cats...

...ts, ravens, decaying leaves, myrrh, copal, death, wheel of fortun...

...riestess, cauldron, mask, besom, apple, pumpkin, fermented food...

... pickled eggs, pickled beets, roasted nuts, rose nuts, apple cid...

..., divination, soul cakes, sugar skulls, jack-o-lanterns, lumina...

...ing, seances, scrying, bonfires, trick-or-treating, mummer's pla...

...t gravesites, delicate memorials, visit nursing homes, samhain...

...gaef, calan gaef, gealach a ruadhain, calan gwaf, kala-goanv...

At Samhain, life and death come together, and with this come many faces of death: gods of war, gods of funereal tradition, and crones that live in comfortable companionship with death. Samhain belongs to all these gods. What you find here is a selection of suggested invocations to connect you to their chthonic nature.

A Prayer to the Morrighan

All hail the Phantom Queen,
bathing, feet spread
to each side of the river Unius.
We salute your lusty nature,
warrior of warriors.
Take pleasure in your tryst with Dagda,
as life and death come together.
May we take heed when we see your raven
marking death and end of year.
May we take heed when we see your wolf—

The wolf may not harm us but we know to fear.

May we take heed when we see your eel

marking a need to retreat.

May we take heed when the red heifer stampedes;

when this happens we know we have lost.

We pray for your favor.

We give you the milk of healing,

the honey of joy.

We ask your wisdom,

that you reveal to us

the spells of your victories—

that your power

travel in our tongues

and that we may draw the peace of the skies

down to the earth

and our battles be won

by the hand of your magick.

A Prayer to the Morrighan for Men

Lady who tricks the wanton warrior,

be merciful;

let us know you on the fields of battle

as well as in the shadows of home.

Should you offer your friendship,
your thighs, and your wisdom
will both be held in high esteem.
You are sovereign; we bow to your skill.

A Prayer to the Morrighan for Women

Warrior woman, free and wild,
stir memories of women of war.
Stir memories of women of death.
We have forgotten these powers
alongside forgetting our wombs
bless the land.
Show us where to reach deep into ourselves,
to find the point between temporary and eternal
to draw power during our moments of struggle.
Lady who transforms
from raven to wolf to eel to heifer,
show us what we must do to transform ourselves,
to live according to truth
and beyond petty rule.

A Prayer to Dagda

Hail to Dagda!

Lusty King, warrior of appetites,

he with stamina enough to please the Morrighan!

We praise your mighty calves!

We praise your mighty arms!

We praise your mighty belly!

We praise your mighty brow!

May you bear your club to defend us;

may those who grant you sanctuary act in good faith;

may you please all women,

befriend all men,

and win every battle.

Hail Dagda!

An Invocation to Cerridwen

Hail to Cerridwen,

mother of wheat!

As the white sow,

you wander the fields;

as the mother of wisdom,

you confer knowledge

unto the worthy.

Be merciful to us
who approach you
in the wavering year—
time itself may be your cauldron,
its ingredients the universe itself.
We are stirred by you,
Wild Crone.
Summon us to wisdom
through the cold dark that lies ahead.

An Invocation to Persephone

Queen of the Dead,
take your throne—
whisper your mercies and judgments
in Hades ear.
Keeper of the pains of women
invisible to the minds of men,
part the veil between maiden and mother;
part the veil between mother and crone—
all are one on this night.
Wavering in the shadows of time, of loss, of sorrow,
rule beside your king.
Send word of us

to our beloved dead—
our thoughts carried to the earth below.

An Invocation to Hecate

Praise to you, queen of all witcheries,
for this glorious night of magick!
Be gentle to us mortal beings—
let us see how we might sharpen our wits,
strengthen our magick,
illuminate our souls.
Long have we been fain to learn all sorcery,
so graciously have you taught us!
We pour libations, raise this toast
to the Keeper of the Keys of Olympus,
to the Queen of All Sorcery,
to the lady who knows the secrets of the gods!

A Prayer to Psyche

Soul of humanity,
woman of the hero's journey!
In you lives all our hope
for love, death, life, and immortality.
In Eros lays the force that moves;

the seed, the spark, the deepest joy.
In you, who labored under
Aphrodite's sharpened eye—
you, eased by gentle Demeter,
so in turn please ease our labors!
We know, through you,
that love endures
through life,
beyond death,
outside of memory.

A Prayer to the Fates

At Samhain, the world undecided,
three ladies weave fine
the filmy veil of night.
Clotho's knee churns the spinning wheel
by which all fortunes emerge;
Lachesis assigns each thread
spewed into her hands,
assigns each vein its place in the great tapestry
wrapping line by line alongside smaller and larger Fates.
Atropos comes to the end, the middle, at bare starts
cuts away, trims, or knots to what binds us here.

We may seek the favor of these Moirae—
a strong warp, a sweet weft,
but once the knot is made
we pray that we be woven of strong fiber.

An Invocation to Janus

Through your maw,
over your teeth,
across your tongue
we walk out the door
into the street.
The hinges swing;
between-things sing.
We walk through you
from old to new
on this Halloween.

An Invocation to Anubis

Hail Anubis!
To your voice do the dead answer!
To your light do the dead return!
To your justice do the dead kneel!
Under your ministrations are the dead preserved!

Open the ways for our beloved;
with kindness lead our dead
to the silent place.
Uphold justice to our ancestors;
we honor your work,
your fairness,
your tender ministrations.

An Invocation to Osiris

Hail to Osiris,
the King returned!
Judge us gently,
lighten our hearts,
refresh our spirits
as your love overflows
like water from the rising Nile!
Sacred light, fill us!

A Prayer to Isis

Blessed Isis,
you have descended and
reclaimed your lover.
In this time between times,

we must live without you—
travel well behind the veil.
We await your return
to see the spark of life
that you hold.
It will give us hope.

An Invocation to the Crone

Queen of Wisdom,
Queen of Night,
Queen who bids
when best to rest,
when best to fight:
gaze with us
into cauldron black!
In the vapors
let us see the future;
let us heal the past!

A Greeting to the Ancestors

As those who have lost close loved ones know, grief is a complicated emotion that mixes in powerful ways with Samhain's reminder of our universal mortality.

Sit at this table

where the beet juice bleeds red on the cloth.

Here, we have a plate for you—

let us serve you, this once.

There, you see the spoon for seconds.

How happy we are

that you made it up the lighted path;

how pleased you could cross veil and threshold

to be with us on this hallowed night.

Pray with us, now,

that your journey be blessed;

that each year you return

until ready for rest.

Ah, but look at us—see our changes!

The seeds planted, leaves nurtured

have branched out.

Some have bolted!

Here is new birth—

new family.

Our hands have crafted, woven, written,

we sometimes feed your memory

with the work of our hands,

the songs of our mouths,

and when you depart,
depart in love—
love unchanged between us
on either side of the veil.

A Prayer to Beloved Departed Elders

Hail matriarchs! Hail patriarchs!
Come here, remember with us,
remember yourselves
as grandmothers, grandfathers,
as mothers, fathers,
as uncles, aunts,
as sisters, brothers,
as daughters, sons.
We remember you with stories
of warriors, of peace makers,
of healers, of teachers,
of farmers, of city builders,
of poets, of philosophers,
of people we loved.
In memories of you
dwell living feeling.
This is your spark, eternal—

an ember cherished,

a light passed from one generation

to the next.

An Invocation to the Young Ones Lost

Barely here, a glimmer, a glimpse,

then off you went

beyond our reach.

The grief for you frees all our pains:

fallen leaves, darkened skies,

failed loves, successful mistakes.

We rail at nature,

so beautiful, ugly, cruel;

we rail at Fate,

at every promise ever made,

and every one broken.

Yes, we even rail at you.

This is grief for the young—

no taste is as bitter

as fruit that withers on the vine untasted;

no sorrow as great as a child lost,

never to know loving touch.

A Prayer for Souls Reincarnated

You are dust, you are wind,

you are water.

You are memory of sons and daughters.

You are in the soil as fodder.

We may not know what form you take

or if you hang amidst the stars.

We just know that you are out there,

that some speck of you is ours.

A Prayer to Witches Gone Before

The words we use

to invoke, bemuse,

have new twists on the tongue.

But you beyond us know

the words of old—

and what you had to do.

Nevermind our quibbles

about right names and power;

guide us to the truth and wisdom

of these hallowed magick hours.

The names we choose,

the quarreling views

are of very little matter—
in what you made,
in the truth reframed,
we know the magick stays the same.

A Prayer for Pets that Passed On

Among the friends we laid to rest
we call our dear companions—pets!
Four legs, eight legs, none at all,
fur, feathers, scales, tiny and tall,
we feel your presence here.
Thank you for the cuddles and licks,
for friendly slithers,
for chirps and kicks.
You have a place in our hearts
that will stay ever after you depart.

A Banishment of Ill Spirits

For those who believe in spirits not necessarily beloved by those
they haunt, the thin veil of Samhain is also a time to do house
cleansing. While the spirits that make life troublesome have
more power at this time, so do mortals—making it an even playing field if you would like to come home to your house in the
order you left it or have nights of uninterrupted sleep.

I sweep you out;
I turn you about,
troublesome spirits,
go to the gods!
Leave here for the rivers,
depart for the skies—
I bid you—fly!
I'll not have you linger
with your venomous trouble.
I'll know if you hang on!
I pry you loose, claw by finger,
command you with this charge:
count every drop of water in every lake,
ocean, river, and sea;
count each grain of rice that ever was,
count every grain that shall ever be;
count every leaf on every tree,
that will fall or that will be.
Never again return—
don't come near me!

An Offering of Peace to the Sidhe

Samhain has a long history of faery lore alongside its legends of love and death. Just as the veil thins between the living and dead, it also thins between the world of mortals and faeries. Some of these beings are mischievous, with no real intention of harm. Some really, really do not like mortals and will eat you if you take a wrong step. Faeries do not think like humans, nor do they share human morality. They can, however, communicate with us. Some modern Pagans attempt to propitiate faeries. Others prefer to avoid them. Since you can't know what type of faery you will get, the following incantation might protect you from damage and convey peaceable intentions.

> Drink this whiskey,
> eat these herbs,
> have this milk
> then go gently on your way.
> Good Folk, we have no quarrels here,
> keep well, far from fear.

An Invocation to Turn Out Bad Faeries

Bane Sidhe—out, away from my door!
You are welcome at my corners and windows no more!
By iron nails,

by rust from rails,
by rowan and peony, primrose, and fennel,
by the metal in my blood—
no more of your evil!
Enough is enough!
By the four directions I turn you about
and cast you out—
my threshold will throw you back with your shadow!
(Adapted from Valerie Worth's *Crone's Book of Words*)

An Invocation for Protection from the Wild Hunt

Ancestors that walk with us,
beloved Dead watching over—
listen for the pounding hooves,
urge us to dive for cover
when the black dogs come a-baying,
when the shadows glide too long and strange.
Lead us into avenues well lit,
to bridges over rivers running fast and loud.
Hide us from the Wild Hunt;
keep us from the hungry gaze of the Harlequin's shroud.

An Invocation for Strength in Facing Winter

The translation of Samhain as "summer's end," means, for many, that difficult days lie ahead as the lack of sun takes its toll on body and mind. In years particularly difficult, it may be a struggle to rally for this day of all days. It is hard to be celebratory in years of grief and struggle. This is a season to express grief, fear, and worries as a means of tapping into this powerful energy to heal or strengthen for what's to come.

> For some the cold grips too deep.
> For others the darkness dims lights within.
> There is ever the mortal dread.
> Treacherous ice!
> Foreign storm!
> Wild weather, too cold, too warm!
> Sleeping earth, let us reach our roots,
> chilling air show us our breath,
> sun shine bright in our memories
> that we may draw you into our skins.
> When the bluster of white covers your hope,
> when days run too close to night—
> nourish us that we may recover
> as the world again becomes bright.

A Prayer After a Bad Year

The bees all died,
the land went dry,
our larders run low to empty.
Hear us cry
to turn the tide—
make the coming years
ones of plenty!

An Accounting of Loss Prayer

Grieve the dead and grieve the living
for endless taking, endless giving.
Free us from the swords of pain,
for what we will never have again.
Money went to debts too high,
once trusted friends said harsh goodbyes,
probably some houseplants died.
We bite our tongues on why? Why? Why?
But still we feel that pressure:
if we complain, to oft, at all,
we may fail some virtuous measure.
Ah, but here we have some time to grieve
as Samhain invites sweet release

to purge ourselves of sorrow.

When sunrise comes, as sure it will,

the weight of loss shall leave at cock-crow.

A Prayer to Bid Goodbye to the Old Year

This holiday represents the new year running into the old one. It is a time of divination in part because the magick of the Samhain season makes it an excellent time to do a few workings to sweeten the future ahead. Bless the land, bless the family, bless yourself, and bless the year ahead.

The balefire flickers out

as the time on the old year ends;

it's the between-hour, without a doubt—

perilous moments 'til we light it again.

Farewell to the trouble,

farewell to the joy,

it all ends just the same:

with mystery shrouded in stories forgot

in the dying of the flames.

A Prayer for a Good Marriage

Should I pull kale
on nights with thin veil?
May I pick one
that brings enduring love:
someone kind,
of compatible mind
who will also treat me well.
To this person I vow
by the sturdy oak bow
in turn I will be kind.

A Samhain Blessing on the Land

May the winds be gentle,
may the bees be blessed,
may water flow free and clean.
May cold pass to heat
in even measure,
for each right month of the year.

An Invocation to Bless the New Year

Hail to the New Year!
We cleanse you with water,

we gift you with beer,

we brighten you with fire,

we smudge your air.

Pass this brightness to all here

that our efforts prove fertile

in living good cheer.

Buoy our spirits,

make the world bright.

Greetings, new annum, on this Samhain night!

An Invocation to Give Greetings to the New Year

Ember warming, growing

'til the spark becomes the flame—

flicker and rise, brighten dark skies.

Your light sends our love to the stars.

The earth leans through that final curve,

where heat and cold make full reverse.

Though the turn be old as time,

our presence rebirths this tilt as new—

yours, and mine.

What meteors lay in earthly wake,

what loved ones will the world forsake,

what precious love will come our way,

all unknown to us on this day.
But in it comes, the good and bad—
the New Year's already burning.
We feed it what we once had
so that the new year feeds fresh yearnings.

A Divination Prayer

Calm my mind,
cool my soul,
send me within
to find what I know.
Open my vision,
lead my heart,
tell me what wisdom
to impart.

A Candle Blessing

Candle to candle,
flame to flame,
I pass this light,
you do the same
against all fear we stand.
Brighter, brighter,

pass the glow—
the higher the flames,
the lighter our loads.
Our burdens lift by sharing our light.
If the candle blows out,
we have our neighbors.
In wind and cold,
we share our labors—
we'll just light up again!

A Meditation to Greet the Dark

All of Samhain—its folklore, its spiritual meanings, its preceding (and succeeding) holidays— creates a psychological conversation between humanity and our relationship with the dark. Longer nights can mean many dangerous things, both because of the cold and because of the advantage darkness gives to predators. Yet it also signifies much-needed periods of rest, moments to heal and meditate that we might not otherwise allow ourselves. This active meditation helps you assess your own relationship with the dark, and to extend your understanding and observation of extended nighttime.

Choose a night in the thirty days prior to Samhain, preferably one that is overcast but not likely to rain. If you have a yard to stand in, that's good, but if you live in a heavily lit area, or do not have a yard, you will need to choose a location where you feel safe standing still at night.

Go to this outdoor space and look up at the darkened sky. Use all your senses to assess the space around you and the space between yourself and the sky. Take several deep breaths. Does it feel crowded or spacious? Is the ground beneath your feet soft or hard? What are the shadows around you doing? Monitor your own reactions and observe thoughts that cross your mind without engaging them. If the clouds part and you get a peek of the night sky, pay attention to any stars you might see or to the timing and color of the moon. Imagine feeling the distance between the top of the cloud and the night sky. Imagine becoming part of the space in between the stars and the earth. Notice, in that imagining, how far apart everything is. As you stand outside, you will likely notice that you are getting a little bit cold.

Bring your attention to the cloud cover. Imagine being the cloud—how the air and light from above might feel, how the air and ground below might feel. Sense the way the molecules move and drift, yet stay close enough together to form shape. Look at the ground around you—are you in an added layer of darkness because the cloud casts a shadow? Look and listen around you for evidence of animal movements and for the movement of the breeze. How is your experience of these things different in nighttime from day? Pay special attention to the way darkness might distort familiar things. Ask yourself, has the night changed this distorted thing or is it only my perception that has changed?

Finally, imagine how someone coming across you might see you at first. Will they know a human being is standing there? What else might that person perceive, cloaked as you are in shadow? How would that perception change based on the direction the person came from or that person's mood or health?

Come back to yourself now, stamp your feet, wiggle your fingers, and shake your head. Once finished, go indoors and enjoy a warm drink, now that you've greeted the dark.

RITUALS
OF
CELEBRATION

$\mathcal{S}$AMHAIN, AS THE most important sabbat in the Wheel of the Year, is a serious affair. That does not mean that you can't have fun with the ritual, but it does mean to treat whatever you invoke or invite with the utmost of respect. It also kicks off seasonal introversion. Many people withdraw from their typical social lives at this time. The taking account at Mabon has become the inner descent at Samhain. The turn of the Wheel to this point turns the reflective toward the spiritual truths within. The ancients believed this time of year a dangerous one—ill-humored faeries, errant spirits, and offended ancestors all posed their risks.

While modern Pagans do not share ancient fears, it seems right to err on the side of caution at Samhain. For many, these cautions include casting circles before beginning rituals, being alert about what and whom they invoke or invite, and making sure elements called receive appropriate release. The circle castings and quarter calls here are mere suggestions; you may wish to restructure them to alter the environment of your ritual or simply to express your own relationship to these concepts.

A Solo Ritual to See Beyond the Veil

Purpose:

This ritual helps you see beyond the veil into the next world. This experience may be different for different people—you may see ancestors and faeries or you could simply see the world in a different way, coming away with a sense of new possibilities. While intended as a solo ritual, you may wish to invite a trusted friend to act as a spotter but this is not required to perform this ritual. If you decide to call a friend, this person should make sure you don't knock anything over, that you do not hurt yourself or anyone else, and that you come back to yourself when the music has finished. Samhain energy is powerful and strange things can happen—it's always good to have a few safety measures set in place because of that!

This ritual is movement based. If you are wheelchair bound or have difficulty with movement, you can also perform this as a meditation with minimal motion. If mobile but prone to stiffness, you may also wish to stretch or follow an exercise program for flexibility before you begin.

Setting:

A place you feel safe. Indoors or outdoors is fine as long as the space is clear, open, and free of furniture or things to trip over.

Supplies:

A mask decorated in any way that speaks to you

Altar decorations such as a cloth (black, orange, or red are all great colors for Samhain)

A black candle (a skull candle is perfect for this, as they naturally lend themselves to magick for changing perceptions)

Matches

Wine, tea, olive oil, or water for libations

A bowl to catch libations

A bookstand or podium to set this book or a copy of the ritual on, to ease its use during the ritual

Calendula, marigold, or chrysanthemum petals, rosemary, mugwort, or wormwood leaves

Towels

A small vial of olive or sunflower oil; you may wish to add pomegranate seeds, myrrh, or frankincense to the oil. (Use this to anoint yourself. The recommended herbs are not necessary, but have the earthy quality appropriate for a Samhain ritual.)

Comfortable clothing

A scarf or other head covering (white or black is best but any color works)

Instrumental music that you enjoy moving to

An athame or wand

Candle snuffers or any other fire safety tools

Pre-Ritual Preparations:

Establish your sacred space before you begin. You will want a place you can dance freely, where any paraphernalia is away from the danger of dancing feet. You may want to wash a dining table and set it up as an altar for this specific purpose. Lay down the cloth and set out the mask, the black or skull candle, a bottle of olive oil, a bowl, bottles of water, and any beverages you wish to use as offerings. You may want to cast the circle at this point.

While traditionally those who cast circles set up a diameter of nine feet, you may wish to cast a circle that surrounds an entire room or floor of your house. Magick circles do not suffer limitations from the laws of physics. You can cast them to overlap with physical space. You may need to push through walls, floors, and ceilings. It is much easier to have your entire home in a circle than it is to perform a movement ritual where you can't necessarily leave the circle.

You can multitask and start this just before you set up your altar: prepare a decoction of calendula, rosemary, and mugwort. Strain the tea and reserve the liquid. Prepare a bath and pour the liquid into the bath, looking to the water and sinking your intention into it. Ask that your daily worries and personal imbalances wash away in the water, so that you may emerge pure and ready for the work ahead.

Dry yourself off, and then anoint yourself with the olive oil in each spot (if your movement is limited, anoint what you can reach):

On the crown of your head, saying, "I connect to the divine."
On the eyelids, saying, "That I see truth clearly."
On the lips, saying, "Only truth may come from my lips."
On the heart, saying, "I know the truth of my heart."
On the belly, saying, "I celebrate the strength of my body in all worlds."
On the knees, saying, "My body upholds me in my path."
On the top of your feet, saying, "I walk in truth and dance with the universe."
On the palm of each hand, saying, "My hands are instruments to create the good."

Stand with legs hip-width apart and arms spread wide and level. Visualize a white light entering your body at the crown and traveling to each anointed point. When you feel yourself glowing, your body moving at each point, put on your ritual clothing. You may wish to add a hat or a scarf—in many religions, a covered head is a sign of respect to deity, and there is anecdotal lore that those newer to practice who invoke Hecate sometimes experience headaches. Wearing a scarf or other head covering can reduce this.

Go to where you set up your ritual. Fix yourself a cup of tea from any leftover mugwort. Turn on some slow music that helps with a spiritual mood. When you have finished the tea and feel adequately relaxed, begin your circle casting if you have not established sacred space already.

The Ritual:

Take up your athame or wand, extending it for raising a circle. Then walk around your designated area three times.

The first time around, say:

> *I take this place to hidden space*
> *between worlds, between veils,*
> *where life and death can interlace.*

The second time around, say:

> *All within this sacred round*
> *is protected, from sky to deep below ground.*

On the third round, say:

> *May all beings that truly see to my good*
> *come guard this circle—come,*

from city, sky, water, or wood!
So mote it be!

If it fits your practice, move on to the quarter calls. Face the east and say:

Hail to the element of air,
to the elementals that make the wind blow and the weather flow,
hail to the guardian of the watchtower of the east, Raphael,
watch over this circle that I may have cause for joy in learning,
and protection from injury.
So mote it be!

Face the south and say:

Hail to the element of fire,
to the elementals that make the fire dance and the heat warm,
hail to the guardian of the watchtower of the south, Michael,
watch over this circle, and protect me from all harm!
So mote it be!

Face the west and say:

Hail to the element of water,
to the elementals that stir from within,

hail to the guardian of the watchtower of the west, Gabriel,
watch over this circle, and guide my awareness
to what will benefit my consciousness!
So mote it be!

Face the north and say:

Hail to the element of earth,
to the elementals that give us our quiet,
hail to the guardian of the watchtower of the north, Uriel,
watch over this circle, and guide me safely through this journey!
So mote it be!

Take a few moments to listen to the noises around you before moving to the invocation. Raise the bottled beverage above the bowl, as though holding it up for someone from the sky to see. Then speak the invocation.

Hail to Hecate, queen of all witchery!
You who keep all secrets,
you who tell all truths.
I accept that to come before you
is to have secrets I keep from myself stripped away.
Dread queen, be gentle with me, if you can—

> *help me to see beyond my world,*
> *to open my avenue of thought,*
> *to let me see what I most need to see*
> *on this night.*

Then pour the libation into the bowl.

Pause now to light the black candle. Gaze at the bottom of the flame for a few seconds, unfocusing your vision for a moment before it snaps back. After you do this a few times, concentrate on the beat of the music playing and the movement it inspires in you. As you feel yourself slipping away from ordinary consciousness into something more profound, don the mask.

Close your eyes for ten seconds, then open them. Dance or sway with the mask on. Imagine that the mask is another person, and that you are seeing through that person's eyes. Look around the room—does it still seem familiar to you? What's different? Observe your thoughts. Do they sound like what you usually think? Observe, as you can, the way your body feels as you move. How is it different from your usual style of movement?

When you have played all the pieces chosen, remove the mask and turn off the music. Sit in the quiet and meditate for a few moments, stretching your body and looking around the room until all seems familiar again. You may need to turn on a light or two to help this process. When you feel completely returned, close the ritual.

Pour out another libation for Hecate, taking a sip yourself before pouring the rest in the bowl, saying:

Blessed queen, Lady Hecate,
you have gifted me with the privilege of seeing beyond myself.
I have walked in your dread world,
and you graciously returned me.
For this, I give thanks.
The rite is done, but the night goes on,
so if you must go I wish you well on your way!
Blessed Be!

From there, release the quarters. Turn to the north and say:

Hail Uriel, guardian of the watchtowers of the north,
to its midnight elementals and to the forces of calm and quiet!
I thank you for your protection and release you on your way!
So mote it be!

Turn to the west and say:

Hail Gabriel, guardian of the watchtowers of the west,
to its twilight elementals and to the forces of depth and feeling!

I thank you for your stirrings and release you on your way!
So mote it be!

Turn to the south and say:

Hail Michael, guardian of the watchtowers of the south,
to its zenith elementals and to the forces of heat and change!
I thank you for your protection and release you on your way!
So mote it be!

Turn to the east and say:

Hail Raphael, guardian of the watchtowers of the east,
to dawntide elements and to that which stirs and whispers!
I thank you for your protection and release you on your way!
So mote it be!

Pick up your athame and open the circle. Take some time to drink water or juice and stretch your muscles. Afterward, find a place to write down or voice record your experience while wearing the mask. What physical sensations did you experience? What were your emotions? What shapes did you see in your mind's eye? During the month of November, you can refer to this experience to build a list of personal symbols and omens.

Samhain Ritual for a Couple

Purpose:

This ritual forms or enhances a psychic connection between yourself and your partner. Aligning this with Samhain makes it especially powerful; the shared experience can create profound intimacy.

Supplies:

A private space where you can perform the ritual uninterrupted

A tray to use as an altar

A black and a white candle

An athame

A cup

Massage oils and sundries that you wish to add

A container filled with water or red wine

Setting:

Indoors, preferably near a fireplace.

Pre-Ritual Preparations:

This ritual involves the Great Rite. While many couples enjoy a physical coupling for this ritual, you can perform it symbolically if your health, morality, or age prevents you from full intercourse. Even if you do elect to perform this in a symbolic manner, take time weeks beforehand to reflect: do you trust your partner? Do you want to expose so much of your inner self to this person? Do you want to see what lives inside of this other being?

Before you begin, lock up any pets and make sure the children can stay with a babysitter. Turn off any phone or device notifications. You may want to put a "do not disturb" sign on your door if you feel safe doing so.

Both of you should bathe beforehand. Wear loose, comfortable clothing. Set out the blanket or rug. Set the tray that serves as an altar, with the candles on the outer edges and the athame and chalice between the candles in the center. Place the black candle on the left and the white candle on the right. You may want to lay down two to ensure comfort. Add a pillow or two if either of you experience discomfort sitting for long periods. Decide between you who should cast the circle, who should call the quarters, and whether one person should perform the invocation or if you should make the invitation together.

The Ritual:

The partner casting the circle should say:

> *This is our time,*
> *this is our place*

at the edge of reality,
where we both feel safe.
The Lord and the Lady
both walk here,
beyond the veil,
free of mortal fear.
Above and below,
within and without,
surrounded we are
in protective clouds.

Next call the quarters. The person calling the quarters should face the east and say:

Hail to the east, to the movement and knowing.
We look to the direction that you are blowing.

Turn to the south and say:

Hail to the south, to the fires on the hill.
We look to you to work our will!

Turn to the west and say:

Hail to the west, to the deep run wells.
We look to you as we work our spells!

Turn to the north and say:

> *Hail to the north, to the darkened earth.*
> *We look to you in death and birth!*

Here one partner should light the candles as the other says the invocation/invitation, or both may speak together.

> *Hail to the Lord and Lady!*
> *We wish you well in your descent,*
> *great mother!*
> *As you know your lover,*
> *shall we know our own!*

The person lighting the candles should pour a splash of wine into the cup as the other person performs the second invocation or say together:

> *Hail to the Morrighan and to Dagda!*
> *We salute you in your coupling this night,*
> *as the confluence of two rivers,*
> *as life and death all come together.*
> *So mote it be!*

Have a moment of silence, to honor the presence of the gods before you begin.

Sit cross-legged, face-to-face. Gaze into one another's eyes. Blink naturally and synchronize your breathing. You may wish to chant, hum, or sing together. You should both have moments of blurred vision. It is okay to blink, look away, and resume the gaze. One partner should say: "I open myself to you." The other should answer, "And I to you."

When you both feel the connection, lay your palms flat against your partner's. Continue to synchronize your breathing and resume the eye gaze. Relax and focus on the moment, on the sound of your breathing, and on any sounds in the background. As you gaze, you may find yourself experiencing emotional responses, visions, or intuitions. Let yourself have them. If you wish to laugh or cry, go ahead. If your partner has this reaction to you, accept it and explore whether you can share in the emotion. Pay close attention to your physical responses as you touch and gaze. Some will be familiar, especially those related to sexual attraction. Others, however, may be new—those will give you deeper information about your partner. Once the response has passed, resume the gaze until you feel that there is no more to discover.

When the physical sensations have stopped, move on to the Great Rite. If you choose to perform this symbolically, have one partner take the athame and the other take the cup.

The one who takes the cup should pour a little wine into the chalice, and take a sip, saying: "This is the love and trust that flows between us." Offer it to your partner, saying "May you never thirst."

The partner with the athame should accept the cup and, taking a sip, say: "May you never thirst," before handing it back. Then the cup-bearing partner should hold it up, as the athame bearer lowers the tip of the blade into the cup and says:

> As the God and the Goddess come together
> in the rite that makes all things,
> as the Morrighan and the Dagda came together
> for the confluence of life with death,
> so we come together in perfect love and perfect trust,
> in this time between time and this space between space.

Remove the athame, wipe off the tip, and then pass the chalice between you until it is empty.

As you pass the chalice between you, talk to each other about your experiences, gazing into one another's eyes. If either of you experience or see something difficult, make it part of the work of the new year to understand this difficulty and to heal or integrate it.

Reserve a little wine until the end. Then, pour out a small amount and raise the glass in a salute.

Say together:

> *To Morrighan and Dagda, to the Lord and the Lady,*
> *with gratitude for your presence here,*
> *and with a loving farewell!*
> *May we never thirst for understanding between us!*

The person who called the quarters should in turn release them. First, turn to the north and say:

> *Hail to the north, where the world lives,*
> *we release you with love! So mote it be!*

Turn to the west and say:

> *Hail to the west, where the worlds meet,*
> *we release you with love! So mote it be!*

Turn to the south and say:

> *Hail to the south, where the bale fires burn!*
> *We release you with love! So mote it be!*

Turn to the east and say:

Hail to the east, where all knowledge lives!
We release you with love! So mote it be!

The person who cast the circle should then open it, saying:

We open the circle now and here,
to greet the year free from fear!
So mote it be!

After the ritual, spend some time planning a few festive activities for the near future. Pick activities where you can talk to one another and share your impressions. Taking a class where you both learn and share a skill will especially reinforce the link forged during this ritual.

The Physical Labyrinth— a Group Trip to the Underworld

Purpose:
This ritual raises awareness of activity beyond the veil, and builds an understanding of why we need death mythologies and chthonic gods. It also draws on labyrinth symbolism and combines it with the popular motif of the haunted house. Each soul that journeys walks a set path that requires the same steps to go inside and out. This makes the labyrinth the symbol of spiritual work.

Setting:

Indoors—you will be putting together a complicated path; best not to struggle with the elements while you're at it!

Supplies:

Costumes—those acting out characters should create their own costumes. Each should allow ease of movement (it's much easier to enter the mind-set of a character when chafing does not distract you).

Indoor space—You may use someone's house, assuming that person can clear all furniture out of the way. Depending on the size of the group, you may need to reserve or rent space in a park building or a church, or even talk to a library or local museum about using their basement or other open space.

A labyrinth template—this will go much more easily if you have the measurements of the room you wish to work with and the template of the labyrinth you wish to use. You can find images of all types of labyrinths on the Internet or in library books.

Masking tape—Use the masking tape to lay down the total path of the labyrinth on the floor.

Dividers—You will need to divide the path through the middle of the labyrinth. Some people use tall cardboard anchored in different ways. Others use elaborately strung clotheslines. You may also want to establish divided paths fashioned from waist-height cardboard boxes and add tall items to obscure the paths as the traveling souls turn each corner.

Flashlights or LED lamps—the guides and the characters should all have some type of illumination. This is part symbolism and part safety measure.

Small altars—there should be an altar at the center of the labyrinth, and then one at every major turn. (Idea borrowed directly from a labyrinth used at Minneapolis Pagan Pride 2013.)

Pre-Ritual Preparations:

This ritual will take extra preparation, from a few days up to a week. Setting it all up will be a lot of work, and usually not something easily done in a few hours. It all depends on the size of the group you have to work with and what space you can obtain for this working. First, pick an underworld. Different ancient cultures had different ideas about what the afterlife looked like and how it changed over time.

In this ritual, part of the group takes the roll of guides in the underworld chosen; others are the souls that come to the dead. You can perform this ritual on a large, theatrical scale or on a small, personal scale.

Those who take the role of a character in the underworld or the role of a guide should have more experience with ritual practice than those who tour the labyrinth. When assuming the role of a specific god or goddess in a ritual context, sometimes the deity represented will manifest his or her personality within the body of the person playing that role. This is called aspecting. While usually not dangerous, it is a good idea to have someone around who stays in normal consciousness to act as a spotter for those assuming archetypal roles. Make sure that those playing characters in the labyrinth also have more experience with altered consciousness and ideally have some experience with Drawing Down the Moon or similar ceremonies.

Those who choose to travel the labyrinth should wear street clothing with pockets—the more pockets the better. Advise them to have at least two coins colored gold or silver and to fill their pockets with buttons, candy, safety pins, small toys, or other oddments. These will be offerings at different points of the labyrinth.

While the following ritual creates a sort of generic underworld/afterlife path to follow, you may wish to create a ritual in accordance with a specific pantheon or theme. Here are a few underworlds you might consider, depending on the heritage shared by your group members and/or their spiritual leanings:

Egyptian: The person who died had to pass different tests
to get to the center of the underworld. At that point, the
soul's heart was weighed. If it was heavier than a feather,

that person was deemed unprepared for the afterlife. E. A. Wallis Budge's *Egyptian Book of the Dead* gave specific details on this process.

Greece: In ancient Greece, the soul traveled to the river Styx and gave the boatman Charon a coin that their loved ones left in the body's mouth or hand. From there, they were ferried to Hades and came before Pluto/Hades's throne. Hades judged each soul. Those that were good went to the Elysian Fields, those that were evil went to Tartarus, a land of eternal punishment.

Norse: In the Viking cultures, they assigned their dead to one of three underworlds: Helheim, Valhalla, or Fólkvangr. While Valhalla was described as a hall of continuous battle, the other lands' purposes were unclear. The Asatru themselves state that they believe that the virtuous will be reunited with their kin in the afterlife and continue to experience fulfillment and challenge, and those who chose lives of excess will face an afterlife of depression and boredom. Modern Asatru see the myths and afterlives as symbolist metaphors. If enough people in your group resonate with the northern pantheon, it may be worth looking for more details on Norse afterlife myth, starting with reading the Poetic Edda.

RITUALS OF CELEBRATION

So long as you preserve the sacred meaning of the ritual, you may also draw from a fictional world that speaks a spiritual truth. *Alice in Wonderland* is often a popular choice for ritual journeys; you may also consider worlds such as Hogwarts from Harry Potter or the shamanic alter-ego world in Neil Gaiman's *Mirror Mask*. You might go space age and create a theme based on your favorite science fiction space travel universe, touring those archetypes placed in the stars upon death.

The ritual that follows serves as a general experiential ritual, focusing on the modern relationship and processes of life and death. This way it does not require a specific investment in belief in afterlife; it will simply be one more way of approaching thought about it. You can make use of the ritual verbatim, or you can see it as a template to help you put together your own culturally or theologically oriented labyrinth.

The Ritual:

Right before the ritual, the person who acts as the tour guide should walk the labyrinth inside and out, smudging with white sage, frankincense, or asperging a tea of camphor and sage onto the path.

The center of the labyrinth should have the main altar. If you are in a place that allows it, set up the table with the representations of the Lord and Lady, a goblet, a beverage, incense, and candles. If the location does not allow candles and incense, use LED candles, and drop scented oil into a shot-glass size portion of rubbing alcohol for a similar scent release.

Right before the ritual, someone acting as priest or priestess should go to the labyrinth center to perform a short prayer/invocation.

One suggested invocation is:

Hail to the elements of nature!
Be gentle here on these paths,
as we are all still learning.
Hail to the living things,
those that live in the in-between!
We greet you in this middle place tonight.
Hail to our ancestors,
to our mighty dead!
Be gentle in what you teach us tonight,
we remember you, and forgive us for grieving our losses —
grief is, after all, part of being alive.
We greet the Goddess, who has descended,
and we greet the God, as we visit him in his realm.
Blessed Be!

From there, the invoking priestess should assume her place. At this point, this ritual template takes the view of what the visitor should see as he or she travels the labyrinth.

Each of the people touring the labyrinth should wait outside as the space is declared sacred. Just outside the entrance, there should be two bowls: one filled with water on the right and the other empty on the left. When the guide appears, he should bid the soul to drop a coin in the empty bowl and then to wash his/her hands in the bowl of water. (If this seems unsanitary, encourage each person to bring his/her own washcloth to dip in the water and then wring out before use.)

As the soul submerges his or her hands in the water, the guide should tell him/her: *"You are water and water is you. When you cross this water, you cross over it and on into the world between veils."*

The traveler should then follow the guide into the labyrinth.

At the first turn, the traveler and guide should meet a Crone. *"How now traveler?"* she should say. The soul should answer, greeting the Crone politely and asking her blessing on his path.

She will then point him round the next bend. *"Go on, you need to talk to your dead first!"*

The traveler may then protest that he or she is dead. If that's the case, the Crone should give him/her an up and down look, snort, and say, *"Hardly!"*

At the next turn, there should be a tray filled with pictures of ancestors or old heroes, decorated with flowers, books, candles, and small heirlooms. Arrange some seating pillows in front of this tray and add a small stack of LED lights.

The guide should nod to the altar. *"Sit down and speak your peace. Your ancestors have been waiting to hear from you. Make sure you light their way before you go."*

Then, the guide should produce an hourglass and set it at the center of the table. *"Get on with it, they haven't got long!"*

Allow the soul to pay respects to his or her ancestor until the hourglass runs out. Then, the guide should snatch it up. *"Along with you! They haven't got all eternity!"* Make sure that the person turns on an LED light and leaves it on the tray.

The traveler should then round another bend or two before coming to a woman shuffling cards. She should say nothing but simply don a blindfold and hold out a fanned deck of tarot cards. The traveler should pick one card, look at it closely, and then return it to the deck.

At the next turn, an antlered man, wearing dark green, holds up a mirror and smiles. *"Look!"* he should bid. *"This is your truth!"* Again, the guide produces the hourglass, and the traveler should gaze upon him or herself in the dimmed labyrinth until the sand has run down.

At the next bend, a person dressed like the Grim Reaper with the scythe should block the path. *"I must speak to the soul,"* the reaper should tell the guide. The guide should stand aside. The reaper should then say to the traveler, *"Come with me."* He should follow the reaper around another bend. The reaper will take him to a table where there is only a jar, paper, markers, and an LED light bright enough to write by.

The reaper should gesture to the table. *"Leave it here,"* the reaper should say, and then stand back. When the soul has named his maladies on a piece of paper and dropped it in the jar, the reaper should say, *"From this point, you must go alone."*

The soul should then follow the path the scythe points. When he/she turns the corner, he will come to the altar at the center of the labyrinth.

The central altar should hold a manual scale, a representation of the Lord and Lady, a bowl, a feather, and a small, heart-shaped charm (better if it is anatomically correct). The feather and the heart should balance on either side of the scale.

A small sign placed in front of the scale should say:

"Meet darkness with your light." An arrow at the end should point to yet another stack of LED tea light candles.

A sign in front of the bowl should say, "To return to the land of the living, something must be left for the land of the dead."

The traveler should decide what to leave in the bowl, whether it's a bit of hair, another coin, a shoelace, a button, or some other memento.

When finished, the soul should proceed down the labyrinth, weaving his or her way back on the opposite side of the path.

As he rounds the corner, a character dressed something like the sphinx should step into his or her path, blocking progress.

"Tell me a story!" the sphinx should demand. "Tell me a story, or I'll give you a riddle!"

When the traveler has told a story or answered a riddle, the sphinx should let that person pass. If the person picks a riddle and answers wrong, then the sphinx should demand a tribute. The tribute can be any random item the person proffers.

At the next bend, the Grandfather should step in the path. "It's time to teach you," he should say. What should follow is a simple lesson for use or mischief—tying a knot, whistling, telling a joke, how to hold a pocketknife properly. It should be short and if the person does not catch on during the first try, the Grandfather should simply smile and say, "It all takes practice. You'll get it." He should then hand the person something from the lesson and send the soul on its way.

Just before the entrance, the Great Mother should step into the path. "To me all things are created, and to me all things shall return," she should say to the soul. She should then anoint that person's head with water and then step aside as that person steps out of the labyrinth and back into the everyday space.

A spotter inside the labyrinth should check in on each of the archetypes every three or four travelers. A spotter outside should guide the travelers to a table away from those who have not entered the labyrinth. The table should have some light, earthy snacks on it (nuts and apples are appropriate).

Set a small notebook and pen at each place at the table, so the traveler may jot down his or her experiences inside the labyrinth, along with any significant insights that came with it.

When the last traveler has completed the journey, the priest or priestess that blessed the maze should asperge the entrance/exit and the center with water, and at the center say:

To the Lord and Lady,
we live in gratitude for what you taught us this night.
To the Mighty Dead, we are honored you have walked with us.
To the forces of nature, we are grateful for your gentleness.
We release each archetype, each spirit, each presence
that came for the night's work,
and we gladly return to ourselves!
So mote it be!

Everyone involved should then sit down to a meal together. After everyone has eaten his or her fill, disassemble the labyrinth. Give any coins to charity or trick-or-treaters. Other odd things the travelers left should go inside a bottle that is then sealed with wax and buried.

Samhain is the serious side of this season. Halloween balances that solemnity with its frivolous, festive nature. One side needs the other to complete our sense of balance in this holiday. This meeting of the playful with the terminal that lends us the strength we need to ride the Wheel of the Year into the dark. October 31 through November marks a season of what we, together, fear the most—the unknown. We don't know if we have all we need to get through the winter. We don't know for sure how harsh winter will be. We don't know exactly when winter will end.

No one really knows what lies beyond life, though a few of us believe we have received a hint or two. Samhain helps us face that by reminding us that we are never alone—our ancestors survived for a long time before we came along, and their memory is still alive to help us continue our own survival.

Happy Halloween and Blessed Samhain!

CORRESPONDENCES
FOR
SAMHAIN

...h, bereavement, ask mentally, courage, beginnings, endings, cha

rnation, wisdom, survival, preservation, hunting, other worlds, ...

ng, release from old bonds, road openings, fire, protection sun

of scorpio, sun sign of scorpio, dark moon, pleiades at highes

t midnight, the crone, the grieving mother, the grieving wife, t

ter, Persephone and Hades, Ereshkigal, Osiris, Janus, Cerr

manes, the Daghda, Hecate, Dis Pater, Hel, Inanna, Is

, Lilith, Macha, Mare, the Morrigan, Osiris, Isis, Pa

Rhiannon, Samana, Teutates, Taranis, the Horned God, the

orange, brown, yellow, grey, green, cedar, dittany of crete, sage

orn, wheat, rye, pumpkins, hazel, hemlock, chrysanthemum, cat

rigold, jet, obsidian, onyx, carnelian, moonstone, iron, black co

s, owls, ravens, decaying leaves, myrrh, copal, death, wheel of

h priestess, cauldron, mask, besom, apple, pumpkin, fermented

raut, pickled eggs, pickled beets, roasted nuts, raw nuts, apple

wood, divination, soul cakes, sugar skulls, jack-o-lanterns, bo

bobbing, seances, scrying, bonfires, trick-or-treating, mummer

n off gravesites, dedicate memorials, visit nursing homes, samh

alan gaef, calan gaef, gealach a ruadhain, calan gaef, kala-

Spiritual Focus and Key Words

Ancestry

beginnings

bereavement

change

courage

death

endings

faerie

hunting

other worlds

preservation

reincarnation

rest

survival

wisdom

Magickal Focus

Confrontation

healing

hope

interdependence

love

preparation

protection

release from old bonds

renewal

Suggested Workings

Divination

needfire

road openings

Astrological Timing and Associated Planets

Sun 15 degrees of Scorpio; sun sign of Scorpio (initiatory); dark
moon; Pleiades at highest point in sky at midnight

Archetypes

FEMALE

The Crone

the Grieving Mother

the Grieving Wife

the Woman in White

The Huntsman
the Husbandsman
the Faery King

The Witch
the Changeling
the Grim Reaper
the Wild Hunt

Deities and Heroes

GODDESSES

Cerridwen (Welsh)

Demeter (Greek)

Ereshkigal (Sumerian)

Hecate (Greek)

Hel (Norse)

Inanna (Sumerian)

Ishtar (Babylonian)

Isis (Egyptian)

Kali (Hindu)

Lilith (Babylonian)

Macha (Irish)

Mari (Feri)

the Morrighan (Irish)
Persephone (Greek)
Pomona (Roman)
Psyche (Greek)
Rhiannon (Welsh)
Samana (Hindu)

GODS
Cernunnos (Celtic)
the Daghda (Irish)
Dis Pater (Roman)
Hades (Greek)
the Horned God
Janus (Roman)
Osiris (Egyptian)
Taranis (Celtic)
Teutates (Celtic)

Colors

Black: Darker half of year, grief, impending winter, mourning, night, protection from evil, sleep

Brown: Ancestors, decay, earth, faery folk, healing, hibernation, nature, roots

Grey: Neutrality, rest, silence, storms, uncrossing, the Veil

Orange: Allies, change, delights, the hearth, inner warmth, sustenance, transformation, transition

Yellow: Change, harmony, health, hope, light, optimism, transition

Silver: The Goddess, the inner self, mirrors, the moon, shadow work

Herbs

Broom: Cleansing, humility, invoking good fortune

Dittany of Crete: Communication, divination

Garlic: Cleansing, protection, purification

Mugwort: Divination, healing, insight, meditation

Myrrh: Cleansing, divination, embalming, funerals, rebirth

Rosemary: Healing, memory, mental stimulation

Sage: Healing, purification, spirituality

Wormwood: Creativity, depth, divination, insight, purification, visions

Yarrow: Courage, endurance, exorcism, healing emotional wounds, the Horned God, wish-making

Trees

Cedar: Preservation, protection, purification

Hazel: Fertility, happy marriage, luck, wisdom

Hemlock (highly poisonous): Astral projection, the Crone, the Veil, wisdom

Flowers
Chrysanthemum: Cheer, friendship, rest
Calendula: Cleansing, purification, restoration, safety
Marigold: The Crone, grief healing, honoring aging, protection

Crystals and Stones
Carnelian: Healing, peace, protection, sexuality
Jet: Absorption, divination, protection from nightmares, reflection, shadows
Moonstone: Balance, divination, feminine influence, the Goddess, healing, hidden knowldege, insight
Obsidian: Depth, divination, grounding
Onyx: Protection, self-defense, self-discipline

Metals
Iron: Protection (especially from faeries)
Silver: Faeries, the Goddess, mirror worlds

Animals, Totems, and Mythical Creatures

Black cats: Associated with witches, superstitions told of magick workers shapeshifting into cats or taking them as spirit familiars

Owls: The dedicated bird of the goddess Athena; nocturnal, especially visible in the late fall season as the trees no longer obscure them on their perches

Ravens: The dedicated bird of the Morrighan who sometimes appears as a raven; believed to represent the souls of the dead and to carry messages from beyond the Veil to the living

Spiders: Associated with the Egyptian goddess Neith as a weaver of fate; webs often used in folk spells, especially for binding troublesome people or for banishing harm from a home

Scents for Oils, Incense, Potpourri, or Just Floating in the Air

Cinnamon

clove

copal

decaying leaves

myrrh

pine needles

warm honey

CORRESPONDENCES FOR SAMHAIN

Tarot Keys
Death
the High Priestess
Wheel of Fortune

Symbols and Tools
Besom: Clearing out old energy, inviting in new
Cauldron: Descending into the underworld and emerging
   changed, transformation
Mask: Assuming a different persona, gaining spiritual insight
   from a dramatic change of persona

Foods
Apple
fermented foods: sauerkraut, picked eggs, pickled beets
pumpkin
raw nuts
roasted nuts

Drinks
Apple cider
lamb's wool

Activities and Traditions of Practice
All types of divination
apple bobbing

bonfires
dumb supper
extra place at the table for ancestors
jack-o'-lanterns
luminaries
mummer's plays
scrying
séances
soul cakes
sugar skulls
trick-or-treating

Acts of Service
Clean off gravesites
dedicate memorials
offering food to the dead
visit nursing homes

Alternative Names for Samhain in Other Pagan Traditions:
Allantide (Celtic)
Calan Gaef (Celtic)
Calan Gwaf (Celtic)
Feast of Mongfind (Celtic)
Gealach a Ruadhain (Celtic)
Kala-Goanv (Celtic)

Nos Calan Coef (Celtic)

Nos Calan Gaef (Celtic)

Nos Cyn Calan Gaual (Celtic)

Nos Galan Gaeof (Celtic)

Oidche Shamhna (Celtic)

Oie Houney (Manx)

Samhainn / Samhuinn (Gaelic)

Samhtheine (Celtic)

Sauin

Third Harvest

Trinouxtion Samonii (Italian)

Holidays or Traditions Occurring During Samhain in the Northern Hemisphere:

RELIGIOUS

All-Holland Day (English)

Autumn Dziady (Slavic)

Boedromion (Hellenic)

Shadowfest (Italian / Stregha)

Triduum of Allhallows

Winter Finding (Norse Heathen)

Diwali (late October / early November, depending on year, Hindu)

All Saints' Day or Hallowmas (November 1, Catholic)

All Souls' Day (November 2, Catholic)

Dia de los Muertos (November 1, Mexican / Catholic)

Day of the Faithful Dead (November 4, Portugal)

Martinmas (November 11, Catholic)

Festival of Hecate Trivia (November 30, Hellenic)

SECULAR

Beggar's Night (Rural United States)

Buy Nothing Day (United States)

Punkie Night (Welsh / Scotch)

Cabbage Night (October 30, Scottish)

Cabbage Stump Night (October 30, Nova Scotian)

Mischief Night (October 30, United Kingdom)

Halloween (October 31)

Hop-tu-Naa (October 31, Manx)

Nutcrack Night (October 31, United Kingdom)

Guy Fawkes Day (November 5, United Kingdom)

Armistice Day (November 11, United States)

Hollantide (November 11, Cornish)

Remembrance Day (November 11, Commonwealth of Nations)

Veteran's Day (November 11, United States)

Thanksgiving (Last Thursday of November, United States)

Holidays or Traditions Occurring during Samhain in the Southern Hemisphere:

RELIGIOUS

Easter and Passover (on years when they take place in
    late April)

Pentecost and Shavuot (on years when they take place in
    late May)

SECULAR

Earth Day (April 22)

Anzac Day (Australia and New Zealand, April 25)

Mother's Day (many Southern Hemisphere countries
    celebrate the second Sunday of May)

FURTHER READING

Books

Bradbury, Ray. *The Halloween Tree*. New York: Yearling, 1999.

———. *Something Wicked This Way Comes*. New York: Avon, 1962.

Campanelli, Pauline. *Ancient Ways: Reclaiming the Pagan Tradition*. St. Paul, MN: Llewellyn Publications, 1991.

Carmichael, Elizabeth, and Chloë Sayer. *The Skeleton at the Feast: The Day of the Dead in Mexico*. Austin, TX: University of Texas Press, 1991.

Country Living. *Happy Halloween: Enchanting Pumpkins and Decorations Plus Lots of Other Spine Tingling Ideas*. New York: Hearst Books, 2009.

Ferguson, Diana. (1996). *The Magickal Year: A Pagan Perspective on the Natural World*. York Beach, ME: Samuel Weiser, 1996.

Irving, Washington. *The Legend of Sleepy Hollow and Other Stories*. New York: Penguin, 2013.

Markale, Jean. *The Pagan Mysteries of Halloween: Celebrating the Dark Half of the Year*. Rochester, VT: Inner Traditions, 2001.

RavenWolf, Silver. *Halloween!* St. Paul, MN: Llewellyn Worldwide, 1999.

Skal, David J. *Death Makes a Holiday: A Cultural History of Halloween*. New York: Bloomsbury, 2002.

Woodfield, Stephanie. *Celtic Lore & Spellcraft of the Dark Goddess*. Woodbury, MN: Llewellyn Worldwide, 2011.

Yeats, William Butler. *Celtic Twilight*. London: Echo Library, 1942.

Online

Burns, Robert. "Halloween." Burns Country. http://www.robertburns.org/works/74.shtml.

Flexner, Hortense King. "All Souls' Night, 1917." Poets.org. http://www.poets.org/poetsorg/poem/all-souls-night-1917.

Poe, Edgar Allan. "Spirits of the Dead." Poetry Foundation. Retrieved August 20, 2014, http://www.poetryfoundation.org/poem/178358.

Riley, James Whitcomb. "Little Orphant Annie." Poetry Archive. Retrieved August 20, 2014, http://www.poetry-archive.com/r/little_orphant_annie.html.

Sandburg, Carl. "Theme in Yellow." Poetry Foundation Retrieved August 20, 2014, http://www.poetryfoundation.org/poem/174308.

Tornquist, L. C. "Day of the Dead in the USA: The Migration and Transformation of a Cultural Phenomenon" by Regina M. Marchi. *Journal for the Scientific Study of Religion*, 49(2010): 771 772. doi: 10.1111/j.1468-5906.2010.01546_1.x.

Wigington, Patti. "Samhain History." Accessed August 19, 2014. http://paganwiccan.about.com/od/samhainoctober31/p/Samhain_History.htm.

Witches' Voice. "Samhain Events 'Round the World…" http://www.witchvox.com/vn/vn_evw/ev_samhain.html.

BIBLIOGRAPHY

Books

Beck, Jane C. "The White Lady of Great Britain and Ireland."
  Folklore 81, no. 4 (Winter 1970): 292–306.

Best, Joel, and Gerald T. Horiuchi. "The Razor Blade in the
  Apple: The Social Construction of Urban Legends." *Social
  Problems* 32, no. 5 (June 1985): 488–499.

Brand, John. *Brand's Popular Antiquities of Great Britain: Faiths
  and Folklore: a Dictionary.* London: Reeves & Turner, 1905.

Campbell, John Gregerson. *Witchcraft & Second Sight in the
  Highlands & Islands of Scotland: Tales and Traditions Collected*

Entirely from Oral Sources. Glasgow: James MacLehose & Sons, 1902.

Chambers, Robert. *Chambers Encyclopedia: A Dictionary of Universal Knowledge*. Vol. X. Philadelphia: J. B. Lipincott, 1912.

Cunningham, Scott. *Cunningham's Encyclopedia of Magickal Herbs*. Woodbury, MN: Llewellyn, 2012.

de la Saussaye, Pierre Daniel. *The Religion of the Teutons*. Vol. III. Translated by Bert J. Vos. New York: Ginn & Company. 1902.

Dickson, Charles. "A Note on Irish Cromleacs." *Ulster Journal of Archaeology* 12, no. 4. (October 1906): 156–159.

Dyer, Thomas Firminger Thiselton. *British Popular Customs Present and Past*. London: George Bell and Sons, 1900.

Folkard, Richard. *Plant Lore, Legends, and Lyrics*. London: Sampson Low, Marston, Searle, and Rivington, 1884.

Galembo, Phyllis. *Dressed for Thrills: 100 Years of Halloween Costumes and Masquerades*. New York: Abrams, 2002.

Gray, Louis Herbert. *The Mythology of All Races*. Vol. III: Celtic Slavic. Boston: Marshall Jones Company, 1918.

Griffin, Robert H., and Ann H. Shurgin. *The Folklore of World Holidays*. Detroit, MI: Gale, 1998.

Hardwick, Charles. *Traditions, Superstitions, and Folklore: Chiefly Lancashire and the North of England*. London: Simpkin, Marshall, & Co., 1872.

Henderson, William. *Notes on the Folklore of the Northern Counties of England and the Borders*. London: W. Satchel, Peyton, 1879.

Hope, Robert Charles. *The Legendary Lore of the Holy Wells of England*. London: Elliot Stock, 1893.

Howard, Michael. *The Sacred Ring: The Pagan Origins of British Folk Festivals & Customs*. Freshfields, Chieveley, Berks: Capall Bann Publishing, 1995.

Hoyt-Goldsmith, Diane. *Day of the Dead: A Mexican-American Celebration*. New York: Holiday House, 1994.

Kelley, Ruth Edna. *The Book of Hallowe'en*. Boston: Lothrop, Lee & Shepard, 1919.

Thomas, Daniel Lindsey, and Lucy Blayneye Thomas. *Kentucky Superstitions*. Princeton, NJ: Princeton University Press, 1920.

MacLean, John Patterson. *An Epitome of the Superstitions of the Highlanders*. Franklin, Ohio: [s.n.], 1917.

Mann, A.T. *The Sacred Language of Trees*. New York: Sterling, 2012.

Morton, Lisa. *The Halloween Encyclopedia*. Jefferson, NC: McFarland, 2003.

———. *Trick or Treat: A History of Halloween*. London: Reaktion Books, 2013.

O'Hanlon, John. *Irish Folk Lore: Traditions and Superstitions of the Country with Humorous Tales*. London: Glasgow: Cameron & Ferguson, 1870.

———. *The Poetical Works of Lageniensis*. Dublin: James Duffy & Co., 1893.

Smiddy, Richard. *The Druids, Ancient Churches, and Round Towers of Ireland*. London: Simpkin, Marshall & Co., 1873.

Squire, Charles. *The Mythology of the British Islands: an Introduction to Celtic Myth, Legend, Poetry, and Romance*. London: Blackie and Son, 1905.

Travers, Len. *Encyclopedia of American Holidays and National Days*. Vol. 2. Westport, CT: Greenwood Press, 2006.

Wilde, Jane Francesca Elgee. *Ancient Legends, Mystic Charms, and Superstitions of Ireland*. London: Ward and Downey, 1887.

Worth, Valerie. *The Crone's Book of Words*. St. Paul, MN: Llewellyn, 1971.

Online

AmericanCatholic. "Solemnity of All Saints." Accessed July 27, 2014. http://www.americancatholic.org/features/saints/saint.aspx?id=1186.

Bonewits, Isaac. *A Neopagan Druid Calendar 2.4.1* Accessed July 31, 2014. http://www.neopagan.net/NeoDruidism Calendar.html.

Celtic Myth and Moonlight. "Samhain." Accessed July 26, 2014. http://www.celticmythmoon.com/holidays .html#Samhain.

Chang, Susan T. "Soul Cakes: Hallowed Offerings for Hungry Ghosts." National Public Radio, October 2007. Accessed July 24, 2014. http://www.npr.org/templates/story/story .php?storyId=15536354.

Church Year. "News and Current Major Holy Days." Accessed July 27, 2014. http://churchyear.net/.

Cuhulain, Kerr. "Satan's Fantasies." Witches' Voice. Accessed November 18, 2014. http://www.witchvox.com/va/dt _article.html?a=cabc&id=4756.

Dennisson, Georgie. "The Spiral Dance through the Years." *Reclaiming Quarterly*. http://www.reclaimingquarterly.org /web/spiraldance/spiral5.html.

Dullahan. "The Dullahan." Accessed November 18, 2014. http://dullahan.com.

Faerywolf, Storm. "Lifting the Veil: Ancestral Magic in the Faery Tradition." *Feri: American Traditional Witchcraft*. http://www.feritradition.com/grimoire/deities/essay _lifting_veil.html.

Fany, Gerson. "Pan de Muerto." *Fine Cooking* 107 (2008) Accessed July 24, 2014. http://www.finecooking.com /recipes/pan-de-muerto.aspx.

Fox, Selena. "Celebrating Samhain." Circle Santuary. https://www.circlesanctuary.org/index.php /celebrating-the-seasons/celebrating-samhain.

Frazer, James George, Sir. *The Golden Bough*. New York: Macmillan, 1922; Bartleby.com, 2000. http://www.bartleby .com/196/.

Gaiman, Neil. "A Modest Proposal (that doesn't actually involve eating anyone)." Neil Gaiman (blog), October 23, 2010. http://journal.neilgaiman.com/2010/10/modest -proposal-that-doesnt-actually.html.

Gray, Elizabeth A. *The Second Battle of Mag Tuired*. Sacred Texts. http://www.sacred-texts.com/neu/cmt/cmteng .htm.

Haggerty, Bridget. "Putting Out the Hare, Putting On the Harvest Knots." Irish Culture and Customs. Accessed December 10, 2013, http://www.irishcultureandcustoms .com/ACustom/AfterHarvest.html.

Johnson, Honor. "Morrighan." The Order of Bards, Ovates & Druids. http://www.druidry.org/library/gods-goddesses /Morrighan.

Johnston, Pamela. "Halloween Misinformation Abounds, Confuses." Fresno Pacific University, October 2007. Accessed August 19, 2014. http://news.fresno .edu/10/15/2007/halloween-misinformation-abounds -confuses.

Jones, Mary. "Samhain." In *Jones's Celtic Encyclopedia,* 2004. http://www.maryjones.us/jce/samhain.html.

Kenyon, Chelsie. "Sugar Skulls: How to Make Sugar Skulls Step-by-step for Dia de los Muertos." About.com. Accessed December 2, 2014. http://mexicanfood.about.com/od /sweetsanddesserts/ss/candyskullhowto.htm.

McCoy, Dan. "Death and the Afterlife. *Norse Mythology.* Accessed July 15, 2014. http://norse-mythology.org /concepts/death-and-the-afterlife/.

Mackenzie, Donald. *Egyptian Myth and Legend* (1907). Accessed November 18, 2014. http://www.sacred-texts .com/egy/eml/eml01.htm.

Mobley, Arlene. "How to Clean and Roast Pumpkin Seeds." *Flour on My Face.* http://flouronmyface.com/2012/10 /how-to-clean-and-roast-pumpkin-seeds.html.

Museum of Art and Archaeology. "Journey to the Field of Reeds: Death and the Afterlife in Ancient Egypt." Accessed July 15, 2014. https://maa.missouri.edu/?q=node/238.

NicDhàna, Kathryn Price, and Erynn Rowan Laurie. "What Do You Do for Samhain?" The CR FAQ: An Introduction to Celtic Reconstructionist Paganism. Accessed July 27, 2014. http://www.paganachd.com/faq/ritual .html#samhain.

Odin's Volk. "Harvestfest / Winter Nights." Accessed July 26,
2014. http://odinsvolk.ca/O.V.A.%20-%20SACRED
%20CALENDER.htm#Winter%20Nights.

Online Etymology Dictionary. "Samhain."
http://etymonline.com/index.php?allowed_in_frame
=0&search=samhain&searchmode=none.

Order of Bards, Ovates & Druids. "Samhain." http://www
.druidry.org/druid-way/teaching-and-practice/druid
-festivals/samhain.

Poland Poland. "All Saints' Day." Accessed July 27, 2014.
http://polandpoland.com/allsaintsday.html.

Recipes 4 Living. "Tremendous Irish Griddle Cakes Recipe."
Accessed July 24, 2014. http://www.recipe4living.com
/recipes/tremendous_irish_griddle_cakes_recipe.htm.

Temperance, Elani. "The Festivals of Early Boedromion."
Baring the Aegis (blog). http://baringtheaegis.blogspot
.com/2013/09/the-festivals-of-early-boedromion.html.

Traditional Witch. "Samhain." Accessed July 31, 2014.
http://www.traditionalwitch.net/_/esoterica/festivals
-sabbats/samhain-r37.

University of Minnesota, Duluth. "Ancient Greece." Accessed
July 15, 2014. http://www.d.umn.edu/~sava0089
/Ancient%20Greece.html.

Vannin, Ellan. "What's the Difference Between Hop tu Naa
and Halloween?" BBC: *Isle of Man.* Last updated October

21, 2010. http://news.bbc.co.uk/local/isleofman/hi /people_and_places/newsid_9102000/9102820.stm.

Villalba, Angela. "Sugar Skull Recipe." Mexican Sugar Skull. Accessed August 19, 2014. http://www.mexicansugarskull .com/sugar_skulls/instructions.html.

Walsh, Jane. "Traditional Colcannon Irish Recipe." Irish Central. Accessed July 21, 2014. http://www.irishcentral .com/culture/food-drink/colcannon-traditional-irish -recipe-118184429-237376811.html.

INDEX

I

About the Author

Diana Rajchel is the author of *Divorcing a Real Witch: for Pagans and the People that Used to Love them.*

She is also the former executive editor for the *Pagan Newswire Collective*, the network founded by Jason Pitzl-Waters of *The Wild Hunt*. She works as a journalist, author, blogger and general creative. She identifies as an eclectic Wiccan with more leanings towards Witch than Wiccan.

Diana has contributed to Llewellyn annuals along with occasional submissions to *Circle Magazine, SageWoman, the Beltane Papers* and *Facing North*. Her writing style is notable among Pagan writers because it almost never begins with a description of a walk in the woods. When it does … look for the rolling head. There always seems to be a rolling head after that.

She is a 3rd degree Wiccan priestess in the Shadowmoon tradition, an American Eclectic Wiccan tradition.

Rajchel lives in San Francisco with her non-Pagan life partner. She is an urban gardener and enjoys bellydance, Pilates, water aerobics, and shamanic dance.

Other Books by Diana Rajchel

Mabon